THE MEAT FREE
MONDAY COOKBOOK

THE MEAT FREE MONDAY COOKBOOK

Foreword by Paul, Mary and Stella McCartney

Edited by Annie Rigg

Photography by Tara Fisher

Kyle Books

For Linda, her family and our army of
dedicated believers who know we can
change things for the better.

———

First published in Great Britain in 2011 by
Kyle Books, an imprint of Kyle Cathie Ltd.
192–198 Vauxhall Bridge Road
London SW1V 1DX
general.enquiries@kylebooks.com
www.kylebooks.co.uk

This paperback edition published in 2016

1 3 5 7 9 10 8 6 4 2

ISBN **978 0 85783 369 3**

© 2011 Meat Free Monday Limited*

Design © 2011 by Kyle Books Limited

Edited by **Judith Hannam, Vicky Orchard
& Danielle Di Michiel**
Editorial assistance by **Laura Foster
& Estella Hung**
Design **heredesign.co.uk**
Photography by **Tara Fisher**
Home economy by **Annie Rigg**
Styling by **Wei Tang**
Production by **David Hearn & Nic Jones**

Meat Free Monday Campaign is hereby identified
as the author of this work in accordance with Section 77 of
the Copyright, Designs and Patents Act 1988 *except for
all recipes acknowledged on page 240

A Cataloguing in Publication record for this title is
available from the British Library.

Printed in China on acid-free paper by C&C Offset Printing Co. , Ltd

Printed on 100% FSC approved paper

A NOTE ON CHEESE

Cheese is often mistakenly thought of as always being
suitable for vegetarians. Many 'hard' cheeses, however,
and some blue ones, are made using rennet, an enzyme
commonly derived from the lining of the stomach of calves.
Vegetarian versions are increasingly available, and are
made with 'microbial enzymes', a synthetically developed
coagulant. Soft cheeses, such as cream cheese and cottage
cheese, are manufactured without rennet. Some cottage
cheeses, however, may contain gelatin, which is derived from
animal sources. All labels should therefore be read carefully.

A NOTE ON THE INDEX

As many people these days are choosing a vegan and/or
gluten-free diet in addition to being vegetarian, we have
indicated in the index where the recipes offer you precisely
these options ('vg' for vegan and 'gf' for gluten free). Many
of the other recipes in the book are also easily adaptable and
there is a list of good vegan alternatives to dairy ingredients
on page 11. When eliminating gluten from your diet, it is
always a good idea to read the label on all food packaging
as there are a few foods and drinks that may contain gluten
without you realising it (e.g. ale, baking powder, barley, beer,
bran, brewer's yeast, brown rice syrup, bulgur, couscous,
dry-roasted nuts, durum, farina, farro, harina, kamut, malt,
malt extract, malt syrup, malt vinegar, matzo, mustard
products, rye, oats, orzo, semolina, spelt, smoke flavouring,
soy sauce, stock cubes/powder, stout, suet, wheat germ
and vegetable gum), so do check to make sure.

CONTENTS

FOREWORD

When I read an article regarding the 2006 report by the United Nations called *Livestock's Long Shadow*, I was mostly interested in the fact that this was coming from an organisation which did not have a vested interest in vegetarianism. It's so easy for people to say 'Well you would say that, wouldn't you?' whenever a discussion of a meat free lifestyle takes place, but here we had an organisation with no such bias informing us that the meat industry was an even bigger contributor to climate change than the whole of the transport industry put together. Not only was I shocked to learn that this was so, I was pleased this was coming from a reputable source that had no vested interests in this argument.

Shortly after hearing about this report, I started writing to influential people (politicians, celebrities, musicians etc.) to make them aware of these surprising facts. I'd also heard that there were people who were advocating the idea of not eating meat for one day of the week. It was suggested by them that if enough people followed this plan, this could have a considerable and favourable effect on our Earth's climate. In fact, the head of the Intergovernmental Panel on Climate Change, Dr Rajendra Pachauri, said: 'Individuals can make a difference... by altering their diets through consuming less meat — say by giving up meat at least one day a week. Reducing meat consumption in this manner will make individuals healthier, as well as the planet.' The respected charity Oxfam was also calling for a reduction in meat and dairy consumption, suggesting that replacing red meat and dairy with vegetables just one day a week could cut an individual's annual emissions by the equivalent of a 1,160-mile car trip.

We then decided as a family to launch the Meat Free Monday campaign in the UK and to try to encourage others round the world to do something similar in their own particular areas. This led to the launch of Meat Free Monday on Monday 15 June 2009 at an event in St James's Park, London, which was attended by a host of interesting and interested people who were willing to help spread the word.

It has emerged that many people like the idea because, firstly, it is not too difficult to do and, secondly, it provides people with a positive way to do something in their own life to benefit the planet's ecology. Many people said that they already ate less meat than they previously had and many realised that they had already unwittingly adopted the idea.

There are other advantages besides being able to help with the problem of climate change. In difficult economic times, people discovered that having at least one meat free day in their week helped their family budget. One of the things we notice is that people sometimes find the idea of a meat free meal a little daunting whereas, in fact, it's often quite simple to put something together. With this in mind, we have asked various people for their suggestions as to what might be a good dish for a meat free day. We hope that you'll find them interesting and easy enough to make and the added attraction of them being healthy and economical will hopefully entice you to try many of them.

The consequence of us all making this effort could be far reaching for us, our children and generations to come. Most of us understand that unless something is done and changes are made, we are going to leave an unhealthy planet for the people of the future to inherit and no doubt they will look back to this point in history and rightly say that we failed to act when things could have been altered for the better.

We feel that the vast majority of people are conscientious and would want to do something in their own lives to help secure a happier future for the generations that follow. Whilst many suggestions offered can be quite difficult to put into practice, the idea of one meat free day per week is something that many people find do-able and something that can be achieved relatively easily.

We hope that this publication and the recipes and ideas in it are something you will find easy enough to incorporate into your own lifestyle and that of your family. If enough of us make this move, we can make a huge difference for the better and set a new pattern for the future of this beautiful planet that we all inhabit.

Meat
Free
Monday

www.meatfreemondays.com

THE MEAT FREE MONDAY CAMPAIGN

The McCartney family has a long history of personal interest in sustainable food — from the Linda McCartney vegetarian food range to Paul's organic farm — but it was reading a 2006 report by the United Nations Food and Agriculture Organization (FAO), *Livestock's Long Shadow*, that crystallised in Paul, Mary and Stella's minds the global importance of making planet-friendly food choices. According to *Livestock's Long Shadow*[1], animal agriculture is 'one of the top two or three most significant contributors to the most serious environmental problems, at every scale from local to global'. On the basis of this alarming fact the family launched the Meat Free Monday campaign in June 2009 to encourage more of us to have at least one meat free day a week as a meaningful way of helping to slow climate change.

What is the link between livestock and the environment? Over the last 50 years there has been a dramatic rise in the amount of meat that people are eating. Between 1961 and 2007 the world population increased by a factor of 2.2[2], but total meat consumption quadrupled, with poultry consumption increasing 10-fold[3]. Due to the vast number of animals involved, the FAO estimates that livestock production is responsible for 14.5 per cent of global greenhouse gas (GHG) emissions[4], with some estimates putting the figure as high as 51 per cent[5]. Greenhouse gases are so called because they rise into the atmosphere, trapping the sun's heat and causing what is commonly referred to as global warming.

The main culprits are carbon dioxide, methane and nitrous oxide. Methane is caused by 'enteric fermentation' — in other words, burping and farting — by cows, sheep and goats, whilst nitrous oxide rises off slurry (manure) pits (primarily on pig farms) or is the byproduct of the production of fertilisers. Carbon dioxide (CO_2) is produced when rainforests are razed to the ground to make way for grazing cattle, or for growing crops to feed to farmed animals. CO_2 may get the most publicity, but the other two are much more powerful greenhouse gases: methane (CH_4) is 21 times more powerful than CO_2 and remains in the atmosphere for 9–14 years, and nitrous oxide (NO) is 310 times more powerful than CO_2 and hangs around for up to 114 years. What this means is that gases that are being released today will continue to degrade the climate for years to come.

As well as pumping GHGs into the atmosphere, animal agriculture sucks up massive amounts of water. The estimated 634 gallons of fresh water required to produce one 5.2 ounce (147g) beefburger would be enough for a four-hour shower[6]. Like fossil fuels, fresh water supplies are running out. The glaciers that are the source of many of the great rivers are melting due to climate change and the Ganges, the Niger and Yellow River are drying up. As they disappear, so does the world's available water.

Reducing one's meat consumption has personal as well as planetary benefits. According to the World Health Organization (WHO) we eat considerably more protein than is necessary or optimal for health — mostly from animal products[7]. A meat-and-dairy-heavy diet is now being linked to some of the world's biggest killer diseases: cancer, heart disease and stroke. A study by the Harvard School of Public Health found that as little as 50g of processed meat a day (the equivalent of one sausage or two bacon rashers) increases the risk of coronary heart disease by 42 per cent and diabetes by 19 per cent[8, 9]. A 2015 report for the WHO's International Agency for Research on Cancer actually categorised cured and processed meat as a group 1 carcinogen, on a par with cigarettes and tobacco[10]. Because of its link to cancer[11], the World Cancer Research Fund recommends we: 'Limit consumption of red meats (such as beef, pork and lamb) and avoid processed meats'[12].

[1] Steinfeld H et al, *Livestock's Long Shadow: Environmental Issues and Options*, Food and Agriculture Organization of the United Nations, Rome, 2006.

[2] *The World at Six Billion*, United Nations Department of Economic and Social Affairs, Population Division, 1999.

[3] FAOSTAT online database: http://faostat.fao.org/default.aspx

[4] Gerber PJ et al, *Tackling climate change through livestock – A global assessment of emissions and mitigation opportunities*, Food and Agriculture Organization of the United Nations, Rome, 2013.

[5] Goodland R and Anhang J, *Livestock and Climate Change: What if the key actors in climate change were pigs, chickens and cows?*, Worldwatch Institute, 2009.

[6] Hoekstra AY and Chapagain AK, *Water footprints of nations: Water use by people as a function of their consumption pattern*, Water Resource Management, 2007, 21(1), pp. 35–48.

[7] *Protein and amino acid requirement in human nutrition*, WHO Technical Report Series No. 935, World Health Organization, 2002, p. 230.

[8] Hu FB et al, *Dietary fat intake and the risk of coronary heart disease in women*, NEJM, 1997, 337(21), pp. 1491–99.

[9] http://www.hsph.harvard.edu/news/press-releases/processed-meats-unprocessed-heart-disease-diabetes

[10] Bouvard V et al, International Agency for Research on Cancer Monograph Working Group, *Carcinogenicity of consumption of red and processed meat*, The Lancet Oncology 16 (16), 2015, pp. 1599–1600

[11] Chao A et al, *Meat Consumption and Risk of Colorectal Cancer*, JAMA, 2005, 293(2), pp. 172–182.

[12] http://www.wcrf.org/int/research-we-fund/cancer-prevention-recommendations/animal-foods

The positive benefits of eating less meat were demonstrated in a study carried out by Oxford University's Department of Public Health on behalf of Friends of the Earth, which found that limiting meat-eating to no more than 3 times a week could prevent 31,000 deaths from heart disease, 9,000 deaths from cancer and 5,000 deaths caused by stroke each year, saving the NHS £1.2bn annually in costs in the process[13].

If you shop and cook cleverly, Meat Free Monday could also help save you money. According to the Office for National Statistics' figures for 2014, the average UK family spends £15.80 a week on meat and fish, with £4.20 and £3.50 being spent on fresh vegetables and fresh fruit respectively[14]. Plant proteins such as dried beans or lentils are typically cheaper than the equivalent amount of animal protein. In fact, most of the world's people eat a mostly meat free diet made up of inexpensive commodities such as beans, rice and corn. Less meat + more veg = save money! In a 2015 survey carried out by YouGov on behalf of Meat Free Monday, 14 per cent of the respondents who were actively reducing their meat consumption, or considering doing so, said the reason was to help their budget[15].

It's worth a mention that eating less meat is also a compassionate choice. In order to keep up with global demand for burgers, bangers, steaks and nuggets, over 60 billion animals are farmed and killed each year[16]. The vast majority are raised in intensive 'factory farms', inside which they are crammed into small, dirty, overcrowded enclosures or cages. The life of a farmed animal is a short and unhappy one, culminating in a bloody end at the slaughterhouse.

And then there's fish: it has been estimated that if current fishing trends continue, there will be no fish left by 2048[17]. Industrialised fishing vessels with their football-pitch sized nets or lines of hooks a mile long trash coral reefs and ocean beds, kill and injure marine wildlife including dolphins, turtles and sea birds, and are pushing the oceans to the brink of environmental collapse.

With so many compelling reasons to have one meat free day each week, it should be seen as a positive, rewarding choice rather than a sacrifice. Meat Free Monday is a fun challenge with an achievable goal that will bring many benefits, whilst giving you the opportunity to broaden your culinary horizons along the way.

Please join this global movement for change because one day a week can make a world of difference.

[13] *Healthy Planet Eating*, Friends of the Earth, October 2010.

[14] Family Spending, 2015 Edition, Office for National Statistics, December 2015.

[15] Meat Free Monday Awareness Survey, Conducted online by YouGov Plc on behalf of Meat Free Monday, September 2015.

[16] FAOSTAT online database, *op. cit.*

[17] Worm B et al, Impacts of Biodiversity Loss on Ocean Ecosystem Services, Science, November 2006, 314, pp. 787–790

A NOTE ON DAIRY AND EGGS

For maximum benefit to the planet, animals and personal health, why not try reducing other animal products on Mondays too? There are over 80 vegan recipes in this book (labelled 'vg' in the index) and many of the other recipes are easily adaptable if you want to mix things up a bit. Meat Free Monday is about changing our eating habits in a small way and making a big difference. It can also be exciting to try something new!

	VEGAN OPTION
Milk	Unsweetened plant-based milk – e.g. nut, coconut, oat, rice or soya milk
Yogurt	Plant-based yogurt – e.g. coconut, oat or soya yogurt
Vegetarian Parmesan	Nutritional yeast powder – adds a cheesy flavour to dishes while boosting vitamin B12
Cream	Unsweetened plant-based cream – e.g. nut, oat or soya cream
Ice-cream	Plant-based ice-cream – such as nut, coconut, oat or soya ice-cream
Eggs	Chickpea flour/gram flour (make a batter by mixing with water) or tofu
Eggs (baking)	Flaxseed (1 tablespoon freshly ground flaxmeal with 3 tablespoons water = 1 egg)
Egg whites	Aquafaba – the liquid found in cans of chickpeas, whisked until fluffy

I

S P R

N G

WEEK 01

BREAKFAST

SOFT-BOILED EGGS WITH ASPARAGUS SOLDIERS

Cook **4–5 asparagus spears** in a large pan of boiling salted water for 3–5 minutes until tender. At the same time, boil **1 organic egg** for 3–4 minutes. Put the egg in an egg cup on a plate. Drain the asparagus and place on the plate alongside the boiled egg. Slice the top off the egg and season with **a pinch of salt** and some **freshly ground black pepper**. Serves 1

PACKED LUNCH

MIDDLE EASTERN TABBOULEH SALAD

Rinse **150g bulgar wheat** with cold water, then place in a bowl. Pour over **400ml boiling water**, cover and leave to stand for 30 minutes. Drain well, using a sieve, and return to the bowl. Add **20g freshly chopped flatleaf parsley**, **20g freshly chopped mint**, **4 finely chopped spring onions**, **¼ peeled, deseeded and finely chopped cucumber** and **3 skinned, deseeded and finely chopped tomatoes** and mix well. Whisk together **3 tablespoons olive oil** and the **juice of 1 lemon** and add **a pinch of salt** and some **freshly ground black pepper**, then stir into the tabbouleh. Serves 2

LUNCH

SWEET POTATO GNOCCHI WITH ROCKET PESTO

Gnocchi are little dumplings that are so light that they float to the surface when cooked. In fact, this is how you know they are done. They are usually made with regular potatoes but basing them on the sweet variety is a delicious alterative. This recipe is surprisingly quick to make, and very filling. Use a classic basil pesto Genovese if you prefer.

625g sweet potatoes, peeled and diced
15g butter
75g plain flour
100g semolina
freshly grated nutmeg
salt and freshly ground black pepper

FOR THE PESTO
50g rocket
2 garlic cloves, crushed
3 tablespoons pine nuts
100ml olive oil

SERVES 4

Cook the sweet potatoes in boiling salted water for 10 minutes or until just tender. Drain and leave to cool.

Place all the ingredients for the pesto in a food-processor or pound with a pestle and mortar to make a coarse paste.

Mash the potatoes in a bowl until smooth. Add the butter, flour, semolina, nutmeg, salt and pepper. Mix to a dough. Divide the dough into four pieces and shape each piece into a long roll about 2cm in diameter. Cut each roll across into equal-size rounds. Bring a large saucepan of salted water to the boil. Drop the gnocchi into the water in batches and cook for 3–5 minutes until they rise to the surface. Remove with a slotted spoon and keep warm while you cook the rest. Once all the gnocchi are cooked, stir in the pesto and serve.

SIDE

SPRING HERB SALAD

Gently mix in a bowl 4 handfuls of leaves: choose from what you can get/grow at home — **lamb's lettuce**, **sorrel (French or Buckler leaf)**, **beetroot tops**, **Little Gem**, and arrange on 4 side plates. Make a dressing from **1 tablespoon hazelnut oil** mixed with **1 tablespoon vegetable oil**, **2 teaspoons white wine vinegar**, a seasoning of **salt** and **freshly ground black pepper** and **1 teaspoon French mustard**. Dress the salad plates, and sprinkle over **fresh spring herbs** such as **dill** or **sweet cicely**. Serves 4

DINNER

SPRING VEGETABLE TARTE FINE

TOM AIKENS

SERVES 4

Dishes don't get much Springier than this. A tarte fine is a thin tart with a flaky filo pastry base. It can be topped with sweet ingredients — apples are a popular option — but here it is provides the base for a light cheesy sauce and a medley of vegetables and herbs. The whole thing is bursting with seasonal freshness.

1 tablespoon freshly chopped chervil
1 tablespoon freshly chopped parsley
60g crème fraîche
2 organic egg yolks
60g Gruyère, grated
6 asparagus spears, thinly sliced lengthways
1 medium courgette, thinly sliced lengthways
80g fresh peas, shelled
60g unsalted butter

8 spring onions, finely chopped
3 sheets of filo pastry
12 large sorrel or spinach leaves
50g baby spinach leaves
80g rocket leaves
salt and freshly ground black pepper

Mix the chervil and parsley with the crème fraîche and egg yolks. Add half the grated Gruyère and season to taste. Set aside.

Bring a pan of salted water to the boil and prepare a bowl of iced water. When the water is boiling, add the slices of asparagus to the water, leave for 10 seconds, then plunge them into the iced water to cool. Repeat with the courgette slices and dry both well on kitchen paper. Cook the peas for 2–3 minutes, then refresh them in iced water and dry on kitchen paper.

Place a shallow pan on low to medium heat and melt half the butter. Add the spring onions, season them with salt and pepper and cook briefly for 2–3 minutes, until just done. Transfer to a plate to cool, then mix them with the egg mixture.

Preheat the oven to 180°C/gas mark 4. Melt the remaining butter. Take a sheet of filo, place it on the baking tray and brush one side with butter. Place another sheet on top, brush with butter, then add the last sheet and brush with butter. Cut the filo into 4 equal rectangles, place another baking tray on top to keep the filo flat and bake for about 15 minutes until golden and crispy. Turn the oven down to 160°C/gas mark 3.

Spread the spring onion and egg mixture over the filo. Add the sorrel and baby spinach leaves, then season with salt and freshly ground black pepper. Add the courgettes, asparagus and peas. Sprinkle over the rest of the Gruyère and bake for 8–10 minutes. Scatter over the rocket and serve immediately.

DESSERT

PINK RHUBARB SORBET

Cut **400g rhubarb** into 2.5cm lengths and put into a heavy-bottomed pan. Add **50ml water**. Gently warm until the juices run, then stir in **150g caster sugar** and the **juice of 1/2 lemon** and simmer, covered, until tender. Tip into a plastic box and freeze, whisking several times as it freezes to break up the ice crystals. Remove from the freezer 15 minutes before serving and leave in the fridge. Serves 4

WEEK 02

BREAKFAST

BLUEBERRY PANCAKES

Sieve **225g plain flour, 3 teaspoons baking powder, a pinch of salt** and **4 tablespoons caster sugar** into a mixing bowl. Make a well in the middle and add **50g melted unsalted butter, 125ml organic milk, 125ml buttermilk, 2 large beaten organic eggs** and **1 teaspoon vanilla extract**. Using a hand whisk, gradually incorporate the wet ingredients into the dry and continue to whisk until smooth. Fold in **150g defrosted frozen blueberries**. Melt **a knob of butter** in a large frying pan over a medium heat, swirling the pan so that the butter coats the bottom of the pan. Drop 4 tablespoons of the pancake batter into the hot pan and cook for 1 minute or until bubbles start to appear on the surface. Flip the pancakes over and cook the other side until golden and well risen. Remove from the pan and keep warm while you cook the remaining batter in the same way. Serve the pancakes in stacks, dusted with **icing sugar, a handful of extra blueberries**, and **a good glug of good-quality maple syrup**. Makes 12

PACKED LUNCH

SPICY FALAFEL WITH TAHINI SAUCE

Take **225g chickpeas** and soak them in cold water overnight, drain and blitz finely in a food-processor. Grind **2 medium onions, 3 finely chopped garlic cloves** and **3 green chillies** together with **a handful of freshly chopped parsley** and mix into the chickpeas, together with **2 teaspoons ground coriander** and **3 teaspoons ground cumin**. Add **1/2 teaspoon baking powder** and **a pinch of sea salt**. Shape the mixture into small round balls and deep-fry in **olive oil** heated to smoking point, turning until the outsides are browned. This Lebanese dish is usually served with Tahiniyeh — Tahini Sauce, made by crushing **2–3 garlic cloves** with **a little salt**, mixing in a little of the **juice of 2 lemons** and beating in **150ml tahini** and a little salt to taste. You can either do this by hand or use a food-processor. Dilute with the balance of the lemon juice and **a little water** until you have the consistency of double cream. Check the seasoning and serve with the falafel. Serves 4

LUNCH

QUINOA AND ROASTED TOMATO SALAD

SERVES 2

Quinoa, a tiny, bead-shaped grain with more protein and dietary fibre than either wheat or rice, is probably one of the world's best kept secrets. Its slightly bitter taste lends this tomato salad a refreshing piquancy that you just won't forget.

6 ripe tomatoes, halved
1/2 garlic clove, finely chopped
1 tablespoon freshly chopped parsley
3 tablespoons olive oil
100g quinoa

1 tablespoon balsamic vinegar
1 red onion, finely chopped
salt and freshly ground black pepper

Preheat the oven to 220°C/gas mark 7. Place the halved tomatoes on a baking tray, cut-side up. Scatter with the chopped garlic and the parsley and drizzle with 1 tablespoon of the olive oil. Season with sea salt and freshly ground black pepper. Place the tray in the oven and roast for 40 minutes until the edges begin to blacken. Meanwhile, cook the quinoa according to the packet instructions, then drain well and place in a bowl. Whisk together the remaining olive oil and the balsamic vinegar, then stir into the quinoa. Lastly, mix in the tomatoes and red onion.

SIDE

GRILLED FIELD MUSHROOMS

Clean **8–12 field mushrooms** of any dirt. Discard the stems and add to a stockpot. Leave the mushrooms in a marinade of **6 tablespoons olive oil, 1 sprig rosemary leaves, 1 tablespoon balsamic vinegar, 2 tablespoons red wine, 1 small chopped onion** and **salt** and **freshly ground black pepper** for 30–45 minutes, turning them occasionally. Grill under a preheated grill for 5 minutes each side, brushing with the marinade juices. Serves 4

DINNER

SPRING VEGETABLE STEW

SERVES 4

If you've got a veg patch or allotment or have just raided the local greengrocer, this is an excellent way to use up some of Spring's bounty. If eating a stew at this time of year seems a bit odd to you, think of it as a thick, nutritious soup.

1 tablespoon olive oil
25g unsalted butter
2 shallots, chopped
1 fat garlic clove, crushed
700ml vegetable stock
400g baby new potatoes, scrubbed and halved if large
12 baby or Chantenay carrots, halved lengthways
8 baby courgettes, trimmed and chopped into large chunks

1 bunch asparagus (approximately 250g), trimmed and sliced into 4cm lengths on the diagonal
1 bunch spring onions, trimmed and sliced into 4cm lengths on the diagonal
150g freshly podded peas
150g freshly podded and skinned broad beans
1 tablespoon freshly chopped tarragon
extra virgin olive oil, for drizzling
a handful of chopped flatleaf parsley
salt and freshly ground black pepper

Heat the olive oil and butter in a large sauté pan. Add the chopped shallots and cook over a medium heat until tender but not coloured. Add the crushed garlic and cook for a further 30 seconds. Add the vegetable stock to the pan and bring to the boil for 5 minutes to reduce slightly. Add the new potatoes. Cook the potatoes for about 10 minutes until just tender.

Meanwhile prepare the other vegetables. Tip the carrots into the pan and cook until al dente. Add the courgettes, asparagus, spring onions, peas, broad beans and tarragon, and cook for a further couple of minutes until tender but still vibrant.

Season to taste with salt and freshly ground black pepper. Ladle the stew into bowls, drizzle with extra virgin olive oil, scatter with flatleaf parsley and serve immediately.

DESSERT

BEST EVER BANANA BREAD

Preheat the oven to 180°C /gas mark 4. Grease and line a 500g loaf tin. Cream **125g butter** and **125g caster sugar** until light and fluffy. Beat in **2 organic eggs**, one at a time. Gently stir in **3 mashed bananas**. Sieve **175g ground rice flour, 50g cornflour, 1 teaspoon mixed spice, 2 teaspoons baking powder** and **¼ teaspoon salt** into the mixture and fold until incorporated. Pour into the loaf tin and bake for 1–1 ½ hours until a skewer inserted into the centre of the loaf comes out clean. Cool on a wire rack. Makes 12 slices

WEEK 03

BREAKFAST

STRAWBERRY AND BANANA SMOOTHIE

Put **250g strawberries** (leaves removed), **1 roughly chopped medium banana**, **300ml semi-skimmed organic milk**, **150ml natural yogurt** and **1 tablespoon runny honey** into a food-processor, blender or smoothie maker. Blend until smooth. Adjust the sweetness, adding a little more honey if you prefer, and pour into serving glasses. Serves 3–4

PACKED LUNCH

HUMMUS AND FLATBREAD

SERVES 4

Homemade hummus puts the shop-bought equivalent in the shade. It's fresher and creamier and you can tailor it exactly to your taste. If you've got a blender, it's also remarkably easy to make.

400g can chickpeas, drained
4 tablespoons tahini
juice of 2 lemons, to taste
4 garlic cloves, crushed
salt

2 tablespoons olive oil
1 teaspoon ground cumin
1 teaspoon ground paprika
1 tablespoon freshly chopped flatleaf parsley

Put the chickpeas in a blender and process to make a thick paste. Tasting as you go, add the tahini, lemon juice, garlic and salt, and blend very thoroughly to a light cream (you may need to add a little water). Drizzle with olive oil and sprinkle with cumin, paprika and parsley. Serve with flatbread.

LUNCH

VEGETARIAN CROQUE MADAME

Preheat the oven to 180°C/gas mark 4. Spread **4 slices of bread of your choice** with **2 teaspoons Dijon mustard**. Top two of the slices with **100g grated Gruyère**, then place the other slices on top to make two sandwiches. Heat **25g butter** in a large frying pan until foaming, add the sandwiches and fry for 2 minutes on each side until golden. Transfer the sandwiches to a baking tray and place in the oven for 5 minutes until the cheese has melted. Meanwhile, fry **2 organic eggs** in the hot pan. Remove the sandwiches from the oven and top each with a fried egg. Serve immediately. Serves 2

SIDE

SWEET AND SOUR CHINESE CABBAGE

Heat **2 tablespoons olive oil** in a heavy-bottomed pan and cook **1 sliced onion** until soft. Stir in **2 tablespoons white wine vinegar**, **2 teaspoons sugar**, **1 tablespoon sambal oelek** (Indonesian chilli sauce) and **6 tablespoons chopped tomatoes** and mix well. Add **750g shredded Chinese cabbage** and **salt** and **freshly ground black pepper**. Cook for 10 minutes with the lid on, stirring occasionally, until the cabbage is tender. Serve hot with **2–3 spring onions** and **1 shredded red chilli** sprinkled over the top. Serves 4

DINNER

CRISPY SPRING ROLLS

SERVES 4

These light, crunchy spring rolls are a million miles from the greasy, tired offerings served up by many takeaways. Making them is a lot of fun — you'll have a real sense of achievement.

225g fresh beansprouts
225g Chinese leaves
115g bamboo shoots
115g button mushrooms
115g carrots
vegetable oil for frying and deep frying
1 teaspoon sugar

1 tablespoon light soy sauce
1 tablespoon rice wine
20 frozen spring roll skins, defrosted
salt and freshly ground black pepper
1 tablespoon plain flour mixed with
　1 tablespoon water

Wash the beansprouts and roughly chop all the other vegetables to the same size. Heat a little oil in a wok until smoking and stir-fry the vegetables for 1 minute, then add the sugar, soy sauce, rice wine and seasoning, and cook for a further 1–2 minutes. Set aside to cool.

Place a teaspoon of the vegetable mixture in the centre of each spring roll skin and roll up neatly, folding in all the corners. Place on a lightly floured plate and brush the upper edges with a little flour/water paste to seal.

Heat enough oil to deep-fry until steaming and drop in the spring rolls for 3–4 minutes, until crispy, cooking in batches. Drain and serve with chilli sauce.

DESSERT

LIMONCELLO AND RICOTTA CHEESECAKE

GINO D'ACAMPO

To make the base put **180g crushed digestive biscuits**, **1/2 teaspoon ground cinnamon** and **80g melted butter** in a large bowl and use your fingertips to create a mixture with the texture of wet breadcrumbs. Grease a 20cm springform cake tin with **1 tablespoon butter**. Press the biscuit mixture firmly over the base of the tin and leave to set in the fridge for 30 minutes. In a large clean bowl, whisk **2 organic egg whites** until stiff, then set aside. Squeeze **the juice of 2 lemons** into a measuring jug or bowl, add **4 tablespoons limoncello** and top up with enough cold water to make 150ml. Sprinkle over **1¹/2 tablespoons agar-agar powder** and leave to soak for 3 minutes. Place the bowl over a pan of simmering water and stir until the agar-agar powder is dissolved. Leave to cool slightly. In another bowl, whisk together **250g ricotta cheese**, **150ml low-fat natural yogurt** and **5 tablespoons runny honey**. Stir in the **zest of 2 lemons** and the limoncello mixture. Gently fold the egg whites into the mixture, pour into the tin and level the surface. Chill for at least 5 hours until set. Remove from the tin and serve. Serves 8

WEEK 04

BREAKFAST

FABULOUS FIBRE MUFFINS

Preheat the oven to 190°C/gas mark 5. Line a 12-hole muffin tin with paper cases. In a bowl mix together **100g bran flakes, 150g plain flour, 25g sultanas, a pinch of salt** and **2 teaspoons baking powder**. In a separate bowl, beat together **50g butter** and **100g soft brown sugar**. Add **1 lightly beaten organic egg** and **1 ripe mashed banana**, beating well after each addition. Add **200ml organic milk**, and continue to beat until you have smooth batter. Stir in the bran flakes and flour mixture. Divide the batter equally among the muffin cases and bake in the oven for 30 minutes or until a wooden skewer inserted in the centre comes out clean. Makes 12

PACKED LUNCH

WALDORF SALAD

Quarter **1 apple**, core, slice thinly and place in a bowl. Add **1 thinly sliced celery stick** and **1 tablespoon chopped toasted walnuts**. Peel and thinly slice **1/2 red onion**, add to the bowl and combine. Whisk together **3 teaspoons olive oil, 1 teaspoon cider vinegar**, season with **sea salt** and **freshly ground black pepper**, pour over the salad and mix well. Serves 1

LUNCH

BRUSCHETTA BROCCOLI DI RAPE

SERVES 2

Bruschetta — it's pronounced 'broos-keta', in case you're wondering — is an Italian recipe consisting of toasted bread rubbed with garlic and drizzled with olive oil. It's usually topped with something else, typically chopped tomatoes and basil. This version, made with purple sprouting broccoli, shows the versatility of the dish. As ever, it's as good as the basic ingredients — you wouldn't want to make this with supermarket sliced white.

8 small heads purple sprouting broccoli
4 slices good white Italian-style bread
2 garlic cloves, crushed
olive oil
1 garlic clove, roughly chopped
salt and freshly ground black pepper

Steam the broccoli for roughly 10 minutes until just tender in a pan of boiling water with a steamer. Cut the broccoli in half lengthways and keep it warm. Then toast the bread slices and rub them with the crushed garlic cloves. Drizzle with a little olive oil and arrange the broccoli pieces on top. Season with a good sprinkling of salt and freshly ground black pepper and the chopped garlic clove. Drizzle with a little more olive oil and serve.

SNACK

MARINATED OLIVES

Heat **1 tablespoon olive oil** in a small pan, add **1 crushed garlic clove**, **½ tablespoon coriander seeds**, **¼ teaspoon chilli flakes** and the **zest of half a lemon**. Warm through until fragrant, then add **100g black and green olives**. Serve at room temperature. Serves 2

DINNER

SPRING RAGOUT OF ARTICHOKE HEARTS, BROAD BEANS, PEAS AND TURNIPS

STEPHANIE ALEXANDER

SERVES 3–4

A ragout is basically a well-seasoned stew. This one takes its flavour from the tarragon, which brings out the best in the array of seasonal vegetables.

8 garlic cloves, whole and unpeeled
1kg broad beans in pods, shelled
ice cubes
60g unsalted butter, chopped
4 trimmed and cooked artichoke hearts, halved or quartered, depending on size
12 baby turnips, peeled

250ml light vegetable stock
500g peas in pods, shelled
2 teaspoons coarsely chopped French tarragon
1 tablespoon finely chopped flatleaf parsley
freshly ground black pepper

Put the garlic in a saucepan and cover with water. Bring slowly to the boil over low-medium heat, then drain. Repeat this process and then slip the skins off each clove and set aside in a bowl.

Refill the saucepan with water and return to the boil over high heat, drop the broad beans into the boiling water for 1 minute only. Immediately drain in a colander and tip into a bowl of ice-cold water. Then double-peel the broad beans. Reserve until needed.

Melt 30g of the butter in a sauté pan over a medium heat. Once it starts to froth add the artichoke pieces, turnips and peeled garlic and sauté until the artichoke pieces become golden flecked with brown. Add the vegetable stock and peas, then cook, covered, for 5 minutes. Uncover, scatter over the broad beans and herbs and shake gently to mix; there should be very little liquid remaining in the pan. If it still looks sloppy increase the heat to high and continue to shake the pan. Add the remaining butter to form a small amount of sauce. Taste for seasoning; there probably won't be any need to add salt. Grind over some black pepper and serve at once.

DESSERT

BANOFFEE PIE

Preheat the oven to 180°C/gas mark 4. Melt **75g butter** in a pan, add **250g crushed digestive biscuits** and stir to combine. Press the biscuit mixture in an even layer over the base of a 20cm springform tin, then chill in a refrigerator until set, about 1 hour. Spread the biscuit base with **400g dulche de leche** or caramel and chill for an hour. Slice **4 bananas** and, reserving 1 banana for decoration, arrange in a layer over the caramel. Whip **350ml double cream** until soft peaks form and spoon over the bananas. Decorate with the remaining banana slices and **50g grated chocolate**. Serves 4–6

WEEK 05

BREAKFAST

PORRIDGE WITH BLUEBERRIES

Pour a **cup of organic milk** and the same of **water** into a saucepan and bring to the boil. Add **1/2 cup of oats**, with **a pinch of salt**, and stir briskly. Simmer for 10–15 minutes or until thickened (the coarser your oats the longer they will take to cook), stirring occasionally. Serve with blueberry compote made from **150g frozen blueberries**, **2 tablespoons caster sugar** and a **squeeze of lemon** simmered for 10 minutes. Serves 2

PACKED LUNCH

BUTTERBEAN AND ROCKET SALAD

Fry **1 small red onion** in **2 tablespoons olive oil**, together with **1 tablespoon fresh thyme leaves**, for about 5 minutes. Drain and rinse **400g can butterbeans**, and stir into the onion until warmed through. Remove from the heat and stir in **50g rocket**. Whisk together a further **2 tablespoons olive oil** and the **juice of 1 lemon**. Pour over the beans, season with **salt** and **freshly ground black pepper**. Serves 2

LUNCH

CAESAR SALAD

SERVES 2

The world's most famous salad was developed in Tijuana, Mexico during the 1920s by Italian restaurateur Caesar Cardini. It proved a big hit among the thirsty Californians who flocked over the border to escape the rigours of Prohibition. Who can blame them? It still boggles the mind that something so delicious can be concocted from such simple ingredients. Cardini's original masterpiece didn't contain anchovies and neither does this excellent vegetarian recipe.

1/2 small ciabatta, cut into large cubes
4 tablespoons olive oil
1 Cos or Romaine lettuce, washed, torn or
    chopped into large pieces
1 large organic egg
1 large garlic clove, crushed

1 tablespoon lime juice
1 teaspoon vegetarian Worcestershire sauce
1 teaspoon Dijon mustard
25g vegetarian Parmesan, coarsely grated
salt and freshly ground black pepper

Preheat the oven to 190°C/gas mark 5. To make the croûtons, toss the ciabatta in 1 1/2 tablespoons oil and season well. Spread on a baking tray and cook until crisp and golden, about 10 minutes.

Place the lettuce in a salad bowl. Place the egg in a pan of cold water and bring to the boil. Boil for 1 minute then plunge the egg into cold water to stop it cooking. Once it is cool enough to handle, crack the egg into a food-processor and add the garlic, lime juice, Worcestershire sauce, mustard and remaining oil. Process well, then add salt and freshly ground black pepper to taste. To serve, pour the dressing over the leaves and add the croûtons and Parmesan. Toss well and serve at once.

SIDE

GLOBE ARTICHOKES WITH BROAD BEANS AND OREGANO

In a large pan add **200g marinated and grilled artichoke hearts**, the **juice of 2 lemons**, **3 tablespoons olive oil**, **1 tablespoon chopped oregano**, **2 crushed garlic cloves** and some **salt** and **freshly ground black pepper**. Cover with cold water and bring to the boil, simmering for just 10 minutes. Add **675g broad beans** and cook until the beans are tender. Sprinkle with **freshly chopped flatleaf parsley** and **a drizzle of olive oil** and serve with **good bread**. Serves 4–6

DINNER

SPINACH TART

SERVES 4

A lot of people are put off spinach as kids, partly because it is a bit strong for some children's palates, partly because it is often murdered in the kitchen and partly because the adults bang on about how healthy it is. If this applies to you, think again. Popeye was right — spinach is good for you, being rich in iron, Vitamin A and antioxidants — but it is also one of the tastiest vegetables around. It goes particularly well with cheese, as in this scrumptious tart.

20cm deep tart tin, lined with shortcrust pastry
250g spinach
50g butter
1 onion, finely chopped
250g Cheddar, grated
2 whole organic eggs, plus 2 yolks
200ml double cream
1 teaspoon French Dijon mustard
salt and freshly ground black pepper

Preheat the oven to 200°C/gas mark 6. Place the pastry case in the oven and bake blind for 10–15 minutes.

Gently cook the spinach with half the butter, until wilted. Remove from the heat and chop finely. Heat the remaining butter and cook the onions until soft. Spread the spinach and onion over the bottom of the pastry case.

Whisk together the cheese, eggs, yolks, cream, mustard and seasoning. Pour over the spinach and onion and return to the oven for 20–30 minutes, until the top is golden. Turn off the heat and leave on the bottom shelf for 5 minutes. Serve with a green salad.

DESSERT

CHERRY SHORTBREAD

Preheat the oven to 180°C/gas mark 4 and line a baking tray with baking parchment. Put **125g plain flour**, **100g ground almonds**, **150g diced unsalted butter**, **75g golden caster sugar** and **a pinch of salt** into the bowl of a food-processor and whizz until it forms a smooth dough. Pulse in **100g dried cherries** and the **finely grated zest of 1 orange** to combine evenly. Turn the dough onto a lightly floured work surface and press into an even layer, about 1cm thick. Using a 7cm cookie cutter, cut out as many circles as possible, then lightly knead the remaining dough and cut out more. Repeat until you have used all the dough. Bake for 20 minutes until lightly coloured or the edges have turned golden. Allow to cool on the tray for 5 minutes before removing to cool completely on a wire rack. Makes about 15 slices

WEEK 06

BREAKFAST

ALCOHOL-FREE PINA COLADA

Place **2 tablespoons coconut milk, 50g pineapple chunks, 175ml organic milk** and **1 teaspoon sugar** in a blender and purée. Pour into a glass and drink. Serves 1–2

PACKED LUNCH

SPICY TOMATO AND BEAN SALAD

Drain and rinse **400g can butterbeans** and place in a mixing bowl. Make a small cross in the base of **500g tomatoes** and tip them into a bowl. Pour hot water over them and leave for 10 seconds. Remove, then when cool enough to handle, slip off the skins. Chop the tomatoes and add to the beans. Place **1 tablespoon sun-dried tomatoes, 1 red chilli, a small bunch of basil** (reserving a few small leaves), **1 garlic clove, 1 tablespoon olive oil** and **1 tablespoon red wine vinegar** in a food-processor then whizz until smooth. Add to the tomatoes and beans, season with **salt** and **freshly ground black pepper** and mix. Serve scattered with **a few small basil leaves**. Serves 2–3

LUNCH

SPAGHETTI OMELETTE

SERVES 2

An unusual way of serving spaghetti that will become a firm favourite. If you like, you can add 50g chopped Fontina to the tomato filling, or if you prefer you can leave out the filling altogether.

2 organic eggs
100g spaghetti
40g butter
2 tablespoons freshly grated
   vegetarian Parmesan

2 tablespoons freshly chopped parsley
4 ripe tomatoes, skinned and deseeded,
   and roughly choppped
salt and freshly ground black pepper

Lightly beat the eggs in a large bowl and season with salt and freshly ground black pepper. Cook the spaghetti in boiling salted water. Drain, return to the pan, and quickly stir in 25g of the butter, the vegetarian Parmesan and chopped parsley, then add to the bowl with the eggs and stir so that the spaghetti is well coated.

Melt the remaining butter in a frying pan. When the butter is foaming, add half the egg and spaghetti mixture and spread level. Top with the chopped tomato and then cover with the remaining egg and spaghetti mixture. Cook on a medium heat for 4–5 minutes, or until almost set. Transfer to a hot grill for a further 3–4 minutes, until golden. Leave to cool slightly then turn out onto a plate and cut into wedges.

SNACK

SPICED PEA DIP

Purée **250g cooked frozen peas** with **2 tablespoons Greek yogurt**, **1 chopped green chilli**, **1 large garlic clove**, **2 teaspoons olive oil**, a squeeze of **lemon juice** and **1 tablespoon freshly chopped mint** to form a chunky paste. Season to taste with **salt** and **freshly ground black pepper**. Serve with **vegetable crudités** and **toasted pitta**. Serves 4

DINNER

SUPER VEGETABLE SALAD

PAUL McCARTNEY

SERVES 4

This is a fantastic salad that can accompany whatever you fancy — here it's served with tofu, but you could just as easily serve it with veggie burger or vegetarian sausages, as well as chips and new or mashed potatoes. You can also vary the steamed vegetables according to what's in season.

28 cherry tomatoes
3 florets of broccoli
12 green beans, cut into 2cm lengths
2 carrots, peeled and siced into 2cm pieces
1 lettuce — I like Romaine
3 spring onions, finely chopped
100g polenta
a handful of chopped herbs of your choice
250g tofu, cut into slices
olive oil for frying

FOR THE DRESSING
2 tablespoons olive oil
1 tablespoon red wine vinegar
1 teaspoon Dijon mustard (optional)
1 teaspoon maple syrup (if you like a bit of sweetness)

Preheat the oven to 200°C/gas mark 6 and roast the cherry tomatoes for 10 minutes.

Cover the bottom of a pan with cold water and place a steamer above it. Put the broccoli, green beans and carrots in the steamer, turn the heat on quite high and steam for about 15 minutes, occasionally prodding the carrots with a fork to see if they are done. Some people like them slightly crunchy, others prefer them a little softer.

While the vegetables are steaming, make a salad with the leaves and spring onions.

Combine the polenta and herbs in a bowl. Heat some olive oil in a frying pan. Dip the tofu in the polenta mixture, then fry until golden.

Whisk together the ingredients for the dressing, but only pour over at the last minute.

Assemble your meal by first putting the salad on the plate, then the warm vegetables and finally the tofu. Pour over the dressing then add a little seasoning sauce such as Braggs or a sauce of your choice.

DESSERT

ALMOND CAKE

Preheat an oven to 180°C/gas mark 4 and line a 15cm round cake tin with greaseproof paper. Cream **115g butter** with **170g golden caster sugar**, then beat in **2 organic egg yolks** and **1 teaspoon vanilla extract**. Fold in **170g sifted self-raising flour** and **1 teaspoon baking powder**, then add **120ml organic milk** and **50g ground almonds**. In a separate bowl, beat **2 organic egg whites** until stiff, then gently fold these into the cake batter. Spoon the mixture into the prepared tin and bake for 40 minutes or until a wooden skewer inserted in the middle comes out clean. Leave to cool, then cut into three horizontally and sandwich with butter icing made by combining **25g butter** with **115g icing sugar**, **1 tablespoon organic milk** and **1 teaspoon vanilla extract**. Makes 6–8 slices

WEEK 07

BREAKFAST

CARAMELISED GRAPEFRUIT

Take **1 red grapefruit** and cut it in half horizontally. Gently remove the segments from the shells, discarding all pith and membranes, and put into a small bowl. Stir in **75g natural yogurt** and then replace the mixture equally into the 2 grapefruit shells (use ramekins if damaged). Sprinkle over **1 tablespoon brown sugar** and pop the grapefruit under a preheated, hot grill for 2–3 minutes until the sugar starts to bubble. Serve immediately. Serves 2

PACKED LUNCH

VIETNAMESE STYLE ROLLS

Soak **50g rice flour pancakes** according to the packet instructions. Remove and leave to cool on some kitchen paper. Soak **25g rice noodles** according to the packet instructions, then drain and cut them into 2cm strips. Grate **2 carrots** and finely chop **½ cucumber**, **1 deseeded red pepper** and **½ iceberg lettuce** into strips. Lay a rice pancake on a board and arrange some of the rice noodles, **grated carrot** and strips of red pepper, cucumber and iceberg lettuce plus **a few coriander leaves** about a third of the way up, leaving a 1cm edge at the side. Fold the sides over the vegetables and then roll up lengthways to make a cigar shape. Repeat with the reamining pancakes. You can store in the fridge, covered with moist kitchen paper for up to a day. To eat, dip each roll in **hoisin, sweet chilli** or **soy sauce** according to your taste. Serves 1–2

LUNCH

HOT MOZZARELLA SANDWICH

SERVES 1

The simple things are often the best and this sandwich is a case in point. The fresher the ingredients you use, the better it will be. The dipping sauce elevates it into something special.

1 ciabatta roll
2 tablespoons pesto sauce
1 ripe tomato, sliced
25g mozzarella, sliced
3 teaspoons olive oil
1 teaspoon balsamic vinegar
a pinch of chilli flakes

Preheat the grill. Cut the ciabatta roll in half and lightly grill on all sides. Spread one half of the roll with the pesto sauce. Layer the other first with the tomato and then the mozzarella slices. Place this half back under the grill until the mozzarella has melted, then sandwich the two halves together. Whisk together the olive oil with the balsamic vinegar and add the chilli flakes and use as a dipping sauce.

SIDE
ROCKET WITH CREAMY MUSTARD SAUCE

In a bowl mix together **1 teaspoon Dijon mustard**, **1 teaspoon wholegrain mustard** and **1 tablespoon crème fraîche**. Mix in **200g rocket** and season to taste with **salt** and **freshly ground black pepper**. Serves 2

DINNER
PORCINI AND CELERY RISOTTO

THEO RANDALL

SERVES 4

Good-quality porcini mushrooms, celery, thyme and a touch of garlic are pretty much all it takes to create this delicious, delicately-flavoured risotto.

50g dried porcini mushrooms
½ head celery, finely chopped
1 small onion, finely chopped
2 tablepoons olive oil
1 garlic clove, finely chopped
400g risotto rice
2 litres vegetable stock
20g butter
handful of freshly grated vegetarian Parmesan
1 teaspoon freshly chopped thyme leaves

Soak the porcini in warm water for 20 minutes. In a pan, sweat the celery and onion in the olive oil until soft but not coloured. Add the garlic and cook for 1 minute, then add the risotto rice, porcini and some stock. Stir until the mixture thickens, then add more stock. Continue the process until the rice is cooked. Stir in the butter, and serve scattered with the vegetarian Parmesan and thyme leaves.

DESSERT
DOUBLE CHOC CRACKLE COOKIES

Preheat the oven to 180°C/gas mark 4 and cover two solid baking trays with baking parchment. Tip **225g chopped dark chocolate (70% cocoa solids)** into a heatproof bowl and place over a pan of barely simmering water; do not allow the bottom of the bowl to touch the water. Allow the chocolate to melt stirring from time to time. Remove from the heat and leave to cool slightly. Cream **125g softened unsalted butter** and **300g soft light brown sugar** until pale and light — this will take about 3 minutes. Gradually add **2 beaten large organic eggs**, mixing well between each addition and then add **1 teaspoon vanilla extract** and the melted chocolate. Sift **150g plain flour**, **50g cocoa, 2 teaspoons baking powder** and **a pinch of salt** into the bowl. Add **2–3 tablespoons organic milk** and **75g white chocolate chips** and mix until thoroughly combined. Cover the bowl and chill the dough for at least 2 hours or until firm. Tip **6 tablespoons icing sugar** into a bowl. Scoop a spoonful of the cookie dough into the palm of your hand and roll into a smooth ball roughly the size of a walnut. Roll the cookie in the icing sugar to coat completely and place on the baking tray. Repeat with the remaining cookie dough arranging the cookies spaced well apart on the baking trays. You will need to bake the cookies in batches. Bake the cookies on the middle shelf of the preheated oven for about 12 minutes until the top is firm but not crisp. Cool the cookies on the baking trays. Makes 30

WEEK 08

BREAKFAST

HUEVOS RANCHEROS

Soften **1/2 onion** in **1 tablespoon olive oil** in a pan. Add **200g canned tomatoes**, **2 teaspoons white wine vinegar, a pinch of dried chilli flakes** and season with **salt**. Cook, stirring occasionally, over a medium heat until thickened, about 20 minutes. Heat **2 soft flour tortillas** in the oven and place on warmed plates. Heat **400g refried beans** in a pan, then spoon onto each of the tortillas and sprinkle with **50g freshly grated Cheddar**. Fry **2 organic eggs** in **1 tablespoon oil** and top each tortilla with 1 egg. Spoon the tomato ranchero sauce over the eggs and serve. Serves 2

PACKED LUNCH

CARROT AND HUMMUS CRUNCH ON SOURDOUGH

NICK SANDLER

Fry **2 coarsely grated large carrots** in a pan with **1 tablespoon olive oil**, **2 chopped garlic cloves, 1/2 chopped red chilli** and **1 teaspoon caraway seeds** over moderate heat for 5–8 minutes, stirring frequently. Cool before using in the sandwich. Cut **4 slices of sourdough bread** or slice **2 sourdough baguettes** with a serrated knife along the middle so they are still connected at the back. Spread **100g hummus** onto the baguettes, followed by the sliced carrots. Remember to scrape in the caraway seeds and chilli. Add **2 tablespoons Greek yogurt** to the baguette in blobs, followed by **a generous handful roughly chopped coriander**. Season with **freshly ground black pepper**. Serves 2

LUNCH

GOOD OLD FASHIONED MACARONI CHEESE

SERVES 6

There's nothing more comforting than a good macaroni cheese. This one doesn't have any superfluous flourishes – it's just an excellent, tried-and-tested version of a classic dish.

450g macaroni
1 tablespoon olive oil
200g stale white bread

FOR THE CHEESE SAUCE
70g butter
70g plain flour
1 teaspoon Dijon mustard
650ml organic milk

100g strong Cheddar, freshly grated
100g Red Leicester, finely grated
70g freshly grated vegetarian Parmesan
salt and freshly ground black pepper

Preheat the oven to 180°C/gas mark 4.

First make the cheese sauce. In a heavy-bottomed saucepan, melt the butter then stir in the flour and cook for 2 minutes. Beat in the mustard, then stir in the milk, whisking as the mixture thickens. Add the three cheeses. Season with salt and freshly ground black pepper and mix well.

Meanwhile, take a large pan of cold water and bring to the boil, add plenty of salt and cook the pasta for about 10 minutes until al dente and drain. Spread the pasta out in a shallow baking dish and pour over the cheese sauce.

To make the breadcrumbs whizz the bread in a food-processor for 10 seconds or grate by hand.

Sprinkle the breadcrumbs over the macaroni and bake in the oven for 30–40 minutes or until the top is golden. Serve with a mixed salad.

SNACK
LABAN BIL BAYD

Crush **3 garlic cloves** with **2 teaspoons dried mint** and some **sea salt**. Take a small pan and melt **50g unsalted butter**, then add the garlic and, stirring often, cook over gentle heat for a couple of minutes. Stabilise **500ml Greek yogurt** by gently beating in **1 organic egg**, then distribute the yogurt into 6 ramekin dishes. Crack **6 organic eggs** into the ramekins and top with the crushed garlic mixture and a seasoning of **freshly ground black pepper**. Bake in a preheated oven at 220°C/gas mark 7, for about 7 minutes until the egg whites are just cooked. Serves 6

DINNER
ASPARAGUS TRAY BAKE

ANNIE BELL

SERVES 4

Locally grown asparagus is one of the great treats of spring. It's only in season for a couple of months but when it comes it comes thick and fast. Great on its own with melted butter it adds a real touch of class to this simple but yummy tray bake.

450g finger-thin asparagus spears
250g puff pastry
150ml crème fraîche
½ teaspoon Dijon mustard
2 tablespoons freshly grated vegetarian
    Parmesan
2 medium organic egg yolks
sea salt and freshly ground black pepper

Preheat the oven to 200°C/gas mark 6. Bring a large pan of salted water to the boil. Trim the asparagus spears where they begin to become woody. Add to the pan, bring back to the boil and cook for 4 minutes. Drain and refresh in cold water. Remove and dry on a tea towel.

Roll the pastry a few millimetres thick into a rectangle 40 x 20cm and trim to neaten the edges — make sure you have a baking tray large enough, otherwise adjust the dimensions accordingly. Lay the pastry on the baking tray. Blend the crème fraîche, mustard, Parmesan, 1 beaten egg yolk and seasoning together in a bowl. Spoon this cream over the pastry so there is a pastry surround of 2cm. Lay on top the asparagus in rows of single spears. Beat the remaining egg yolk and paint the pastry borders. Bake the tart for 30 minutes.

Serve 5 minutes out of the oven, though it is excellent cold.

DESSERT
LEMON AND PISTACHIO BISCOTTI

Preheat the oven to 180°C/gas mark 4. In a mixing bowl, place **250g plain flour, 1 teaspoon baking powder, 175g caster sugar, a pinch of salt, 2 organic eggs, grated zest of 3 lemons, 1 tablespoon lemon juice, 100g blanched almonds, toasted and chopped**, and **50g chopped pistachios**. Mix to form a firm dough. Roll into a ball, cut in half and roll each portion into a sausage shape before placing on a lightly floured baking tray. Place in the preheated oven for 10 minutes until golden. Remove from the oven, cool for 10 minutes, then use a serrated knife to cut into diagonal slices 1cm thick. Arrange the slices on the baking tray and return to the oven for a further 15 minutes until slightly golden. Transfer to a wire rack to cool and crisp up. Makes 16

WEEK 09

BREAKFAST

CREPES WITH LEMON AND SUGAR

Sift **125g plain flour** and **a pinch of salt** into a bowl. Add **1 organic egg** and gradually beat in **150ml organic milk**. Add another **150ml milk** and beat until smooth. Lightly oil a frying pan and place over a moderate heat. Pour in just enough batter to cover the base of the pan. Cook until the underside is golden, then turn and cook the other side. Repeat with the remaining batter. To serve sprinkle with **lemon juice**, roll up and top with a sprinkling of **sugar**. Makes 8–10

PACKED LUNCH

VEGETABLE PILAU

In a large saucepan, soften **1 finely chopped medium onion** and **1 crushed garlic clove** in **1 tablespoon corn oil**, then add **2 teaspoons ground cardamom**, **1 teaspoon ground turmeric**, **1 teaspoon ground cinnamon** and fry for 1 minute. Break up **100g cauliflower florets** into tiny pieces, and add to the pan with **100g frozen peas** and **50g sultanas**. Stir for half a minute, then add **175g rinsed basmati rice** and **300ml water**. Bring to the boil, stirring occasionally. Cover with a tight-fitting lid and simmer for 15 minutes. Stir occasionally, adding a little more warm water during cooking if necessary. Serves 4

LUNCH

CREAMY BROCCOLI SOUP

LAURA AND WOODY HARRELSON

It'd be hard not to love any recipe devised by Woody Harrelson, star of Cheers and numerous Hollywood movies. This soup comes highly recommended. It's creamy but it doesn't have any cream in it and it's incredibly easy to make.

650g red potatoes, diced into cubes
1kg broccoli, chopped into small florets
220g leeks, trimmed and roughly chopped
1 garlic clove
1.8 litres water
4 tablespoons olive oil
3 cubes vegetable bouillon
2 teaspoons Himalayan salt (or table salt
   if you can't find this)
freshly ground black pepper to taste

SERVES 8

Prepare the vegetables and steam the potatoes and broccoli until tender (approximately 15–20 minutes). Cook the leeks in a small amount of water until tender. Place half the vegetable mixture, 1 litre of the water and the rest of the ingredients (except the olive oil) in a high powered blender. Build power up to the highest level. At that point, slowly pour 2 tablespoons of the olive oil into the mixture. Blend until smooth. Pour the mixture into a large pot and start warming it over a low heat. Blend the remaining vegetable mixture and water and repeat the slow addition of the oil while blending at the highest speed. Add to the pot and stir every few minutes while warming the soup to desired temperature. Serve hot.

SIDE
GARLIC BREAD

Preheat the oven to 180°C/gas mark 4. Make diagonal cuts along **1 long French stick** at about 2.5cm intervals — cut well into the bread but don't slice all the way through. Soften **85g butter** in a small pan and stir in **2 crushed garlic cloves** and **1 teaspoon freshly chopped parsley**. Brush the garlic butter on each side of each cut in the bread until it is all used up. Wrap the whole French stick in baking foil and heat it through for 10 minutes. Unwrap and serve immediately. Serves 3–4

DINNER
LINGUINE WITH ALMONDS AND CACIOCAVALLO

MARIO BATALI

SERVES 8

Mozzarella and Parmesan are rightly famous but it's sometimes good to cook with one of Italy's other excellent cheeses. Caciocavallo is a speciality of the south, made by repeatedly stretching and pulling raw cow's milk curd. It comes in a distinctive gourd shape and is hung up to dry by a string tied around the neck. The almonds and red pepper flakes are also typical of Southern Italy and give this recipe its nuttiness and bite.

110ml extra virgin olive oil
6 garlic cloves, thinly sliced
1 tablespoon dried chilli flakes
110g sliced blanched almonds, chopped
salt
700g linguine fini
3 tablespoons finely chopped fresh parsley
110g freshly grated Caciocavallo

Bring 8 litres of water to a boil in a large pasta pot. While the water is heating, heat the oil in a large sauté pan over medium heat. Add the garlic and cook until it is light brown. Add the dried chilli and the almonds, and cook until the almonds are light golden brown, 2–3 minutes. Remove from the heat.

Add 2 tablespoons salt to the boiling water. Drop the linguine into the water and cook for 1 minute less than the packet instructions indicate. Just before the pasta is done, carefully ladle 55ml of the cooking water into the pan containing the almonds.

Drain the pasta in a colander, and add it to the almond sauce. Add the parsley and toss over medium heat for about 30 seconds, until the pasta is nicely coated. Then remove from the heat, add half the cheese, and toss like a salad for 15 seconds. Pour into a warmed serving bowl and serve immediately with the remaining cheese on the side.

DESSERT
CASSATA

Put **300g vanilla ice cream** in a mixing bowl. Allow to soften slightly. Crumble **75g amaretti biscuits** into the ice cream and add **100g mixed dried fruit** and **25g toasted flaked almonds**. Gently mix to incorporate all the ingredients. Pile into a small freezerproof bowl or ice cream container and place in the coldest part of the freezer for 1 hour. Melt **50g plain chocolate** in a heatproof bowl over a pan of gently simmering water. Remove from the heat. When ready to serve, scoop the ice cream onto chilled serving plates and drizzle with the melted chocolate. Serve immediately. Serves 4

WEEK 10

BREAKFAST
FRUIT AND NUT BREAKFAST BARS

Preheat the oven to 180°C/gas mark 4. Grease and line a baking tin measuring 20 x 30cm. Melt **50g butter** and **200g runny honey** in a saucepan. Add **225g rolled oats**, **50g sunflower seeds**, **50g pumpkin seeds**, **50g chopped almonds**, **50g chopped hazelnuts** and **100g chopped dates** and **100g dried apricots** and mix together really well. Spoon into the prepared tin and bake for 20 minutes or until golden brown. Remove from the oven and leave to cool completely before turning out of the tin. Cut into rectangles or squares. The bars will keep for a week in an airtight container. Makes 16 bars

PACKED LUNCH
PASTA WITH FRESH SPRING HERBS

Cook **350g spaghetti or macaroni** until tender, rinse under cold water and drain. Mix **3 tablespoons freshly chopped parsley**, **3 tablespoons freshly chopped basil**, **1 tablespoon freshly chopped oregano**, **1 crushed garlic clove**, **90ml olive oil** and **225g cottage cheese** in a blender and liquidise to make a sauce. Add the sauce to the cooked pasta and gently heat, while stirring. Serves 4

LUNCH
CRUNCHY CAULIFLOWER AND MACARONI

Nothing beats a good cauliflower cheese, except possibly a good macaroni cheese. This dish combines the best of both. It's also a doddle to make.

1 cauliflower, chopped into small florets
125g macaroni
50g butter
125g mushrooms, sliced
25g plain flour
300ml organic milk, heated just to boiling point
50g Red Leicester, grated
2 tablespoons dry breadcrumbs
salt and freshly ground black pepper

SERVES 4

Cook the cauliflower florets in boiling water for 5–10 minutes until just tender. Drain. While the cauliflower is cooking, cook the macaroni according to the packet instructions. Drain.

Melt the butter in a third large saucepan and fry the mushrooms until they are soft. Stir in the flour until you have a glossy paste. Cook for 1 minute. Pour in the hot milk, a little at a time, and whisk vigorously until the milk has been incorporated. Keep adding the milk, continuing to whisk, until it has all been added and you have a smooth, glossy, creamy, mushroom sauce.

Stir in the cauliflower, macaroni and salt and pepper to taste. Preheat the grill to hot. Spoon the mixture into a shallow, heatproof dish.

Sprinkle over the cheese and breadcrumbs and brown lightly under the grill. Carefully remove the dish using oven gloves and serve at once.

SIDE
GREEN BEANS WITH FENUGREEK BUTTER

Cook **200g fine green beans** in boiling salted water for 5–10 minutes until tender but still crunchy. Drain and set aside. Melt **25g butter** in the saucepan and stir in the **juice of 1 lime**, **20g finely chopped fresh coriander** and **1 teaspoon ground fenugreek**. Tip in the beans and shake the pan to cover them with the butter. Season to taste and serve immediately. Serves 2–4

DINNER
STIR-FRY WITH SPRING VEG AND NOODLES

Stir-fries always seem to go down well and they are quick and easy to make. The broccoli and pak choi in this one provide freshness and bite, while the broad beans add a note of pungency. Feel free to incorporate other spring vegetables if you fancy.

250g noodles of your choice
1 tablespoon vegetable oil
250g purple sprouting broccoli or tenderstem, cut into small florets
4 garlic cloves, finely chopped
1cm piece root ginger, finely chopped
1 red chilli, deseeded and finely sliced

1 bunch spring onions, sliced
140g broad beans (600g unshelled weight), cooked and peeled of outer skins if large
2 heads pak choi, cut into eighths
1 1/2 tablespoons hoisin sauce
1 tablespoon soy sauce (add extra to suit your own taste)

SERVES 4

Bring a large saucepan of water to the boil and cook the noodles according to the packet instructions, or until just tender. Drain well and rinse with cold water.

Heat the oil in a non-stick wok. Add the broccoli, then fry on a high heat for 5 minutes or until just tender, adding a little water if it begins to catch. Add the garlic, ginger and chilli, fry for a further minute, then toss through the spring onions, broad beans and pak choi. Stir-fry for 2–3 minutes. Add the hoisin and soy sauces and warm through. Toss the noodles in with the vegetables and serve.

DESSERT
LEMON AND LIME TART

Prepare the pastry by adding **200g plain flour**, **125g diced butter**, **50g icing sugar** and a pinch of **salt** into the bowl of a food-processor. Use the pulse button to rub the butter into the flour until the mixture resembles fine breadcrumbs. Mix **2 large organic egg yolks** with **1 tablespoon cold water**, add to the flour mixture and pulse again until the a dough starts to form. Lightly shape the dough into a smooth ball, flatten into a disc, cover with clingfilm and chill for an hour until firm. Lightly dust a work surface with flour, roll out the dough into a disc and use to line a 23cm springform tart tin. Prick the base with a fork and chill the pastry again for 20 minutes. Preheat the oven to 190°C/gas mark 5 and place a solid baking tray on the middle shelf of the oven. Line the pastry shell with baking parchment and baking beans or rice and cook on the hot baking tray for 15–20 minutes until pale golden. Remove from the oven and cool slightly while you prepare the filling and turn the oven down to 150°C/gas mark 2. Finely grate the zest from **1 lemon** and **1 lime** into a bowl and squeeze the juice from **2 lemons** and **3 limes**. Set aside. Whisk **6 large organic eggs** and **250g caster sugar** together in a large bowl, add **150ml double cream**, mix to combine and add the lemon and lime juice. Strain into a large measuring jug, add the grated zests and stir to combine. Pour the mixture into the baked pastry case and carefully slide the baking tray back into the oven and bake for 30–40 minutes until the centre is only just set. Remove from the oven and leave to cool to room temperature. Dust the top with **icing sugar** and, if desired, caramelise to a light amber colour using a blow torch. Serve at room temperature. Makes 10–12 slices

WEEK 11

BREAKFAST

BREAKFAST BRIOCHE

Cut **4 slices of brioche**, spread with **3 tablespoons apricot jam** and sandwich together. Whisk together **2 organic eggs, 25g sugar** and **50ml organic milk**. Melt **15g butter** in a frying pan. Dip the brioche sandwiches in the egg mixture and fry for 2 minutes on each side until golden brown. Serves 2

PACKED LUNCH

MELON, LIME AND MINT SOUP

STEFAN GATES

Cut **3 chilled ripe melons** in half, scoop out the pips and discard. Scoop the flesh out of the melons and put in a food-processor with **200ml orange juice**, the **juice of 1 lime**, **a pinch of salt**, **1 teaspoon sugar** and **a few fresh mint leaves**. Whizz until smooth — if the mixture is too stiff, add a little more orange juice. If you kept the melons in the fridge you can serve the soup straight away. If not, refrigerate for about 30 minutes. Scatter the **zest of 1 lime** and **some fresh mint leaves** on top just before serving. Serves 6

LUNCH

PAD THAI NOODLES

This is the classic dish of Thailand, sometimes served as accompaniment to other food but more than good enough to eat on its own. It is a riot of textures and flavours, from the crunch of the peanuts to the tartness of the tamarind and the smoothness of the noodles.

125g medium rice noodles
1 teaspoon tamarind paste
1 1/2 tablespoons vegetarian oyster sauce
1 teaspoon sugar
1 garlic clove, finely chopped
2 spring onions, cut into thin slices about 1cm

1 red chilli, deseeded and finely chopped
1 organic egg
50g beansprouts
a handful of peanuts, chopped
a handful of coriander leaves
wedges of lime

SERVES 2

Tip the noodles into a large bowl and cover with boiling water. Leave to stand for 5–10 minutes until the noodles are soft, then drain well. (You can do this part ahead of time — then just run the noodles under cold water until cool, and toss through a little oil to stop them from sticking.)

Next, mix together the tamarind paste, vegetarian oyster sauce and sugar in a small bowl.

Heat a wok or large frying pan over a high heat. Add the garlic, spring onions and chilli. Toss the ingredients around the wok so they are constantly moving. Cook for 30 seconds, until they begin to soften. Push the vegetables to the sides of the wok, then crack the egg into the centre. Keep stirring the egg for 30 seconds until it begins to set and resembles a broken-up omelette. Add the beansprouts, followed by the noodles, then pour over the sauce mixture. Toss everything together and heat through. Spoon out onto plates. Serve with the chopped peanuts and coriander leaves sprinkled over the top and wedges of lime on the side.

SIDE
CANNELLINI BEAN AND ASPARAGUS GRATIN

Preheat the oven to 180°C/gas mark 4. Sauté **1/2 chopped onion** and **2 crushed garlic cloves** in olive oil until tender. Add **1 bunch asparagus cut into 2.5cm pieces** and season with **salt** and **freshly ground black pepper**. Stir in **100g cooked cannellini beans** and set aside. Sauté the other **1/2 chopped onion** in **1 tablespoon butter**, then add **100g breadcrumbs**. Place the bean and asparagus mixture in a buttered baking dish, dot a few tablespoons of **ricotta** over the mixture and top with the breadcrumbs. Bake for 15 minutes, or until the breadcrumb topping is golden brown and crusty. Serves 4

DINNER
SPINACH, RICOTTA AND PARMESAN GNOCCHI WITH TOMATO SAUCE

SERVES 4

Here's another mouth-watering variation on the gnocchi theme (see Spring, Week 1, Lunch). This time, the base vegetable is spinach, which gives these mini-dumplings their pleasing green colour. The tomato sauce recipe is a classic – you may find it comes in useful in other contexts.

FOR THE GNOCCHI
500g fresh spinach, discard any tough stalks
25g butter
1 onion, finely chopped
freshly grated nutmeg
150g ricotta
125g freshly grated vegetarian Parmesan
60g plain flour, plus extra for dusting
2 large organic egg yolks
salt and freshly ground black pepper

FOR THE TOMATO SAUCE
1 tablespoon olive oil
1 fat clove of garlic, crushed
400g can tomatoes
1 teaspoon caster sugar
1 tablespoon freshly chopped basil leaves
salt and freshly ground black pepper

TO SERVE
freshly grated vegetarian Parmesan
extra virgin olive oil

Tip the spinach into a large pan over a medium heat and cook until the leaves are wilted and tender. Drain and leave until cool enough to handle, then squeeze the spinach between your hands to remove as much water as possible and roughly chop.

Melt the butter in a sauté pan, add a quarter of the chopped onion and cook over a medium heat until tender but not coloured. Add the chopped spinach and cook for a further 2 minutes. Tip into a bowl, season with freshly grated nutmeg, salt and black pepper and leave to cool. Add the ricotta, Parmesan, plain flour and egg yolks to the mixture and mix until smooth. Cover and chill the mixture for a couple of hours to firm up.

Meanwhile prepare the tomato sauce. Heat the olive oil in a saucepan over a medium heat, add the remaining onion and cook until soft but not coloured. Add the crushed garlic and cook for a further minute. Add the canned tomatoes, caster sugar and season well with salt and freshly ground black pepper. Bring to the boil and simmer over a medium heat for about 7 minutes until slightly thickened. Add the chopped basil.

Lightly dust the work surface with a little plain flour and roll the spinach mixture into a log about 3cm in diameter. Cut the log into 3cm pillows or gnocchi and lay on a baking tray that has been lightly dusted with plain flour. Bring a large pan of salted water to the boil. Add the gnocchi and cook for about 3 minutes until tender and the gnocchi float to the surface of the water. Drain the gnocchi and serve in bowls with the tomato sauce, scattered with grated Parmesan and drizzled with extra virgin olive oil. ̈

DESSERT
GOOSEBERRY FOOL

Put **300g topped and tailed gooseberries** in a pan with **2 tablespoons caster sugar** and **2 tablespoons water**. Gently stew until the gooseberries are soft and pulpy. Set aside and leave to cool. Once cooled add half the gooseberry mixture to **100g Greek yogurt** and mix together. Take 6 glasses and fill with the gooseberry yogurt mixture and top with the remaining stewed gooseberries. Decorate with **whole poached gooseberries**, if you wish. Serves 6

WEEK 12

BREAKFAST

FRIED BANANAS WITH PECANS AND MAPLE SYRUP

Halve **2 bananas** lengthways and sprinkle over the juice of **1/2 lemon**. Melt **25g butter** in a frying pan, add the bananas, cook until browned on both sides, then transfer to warm plates. Add **25g chopped pecans** to the pan and cook until lightly toasted. Stir in **2 tablespoons maple syrup** and heat through. Pour over the bananas and serve at once on their own or with yogurt. Serves 2

PACKED LUNCH

TANGY CAULIFLOWER PICKLE AND CHEESE SANDWICH

This pickle is incredibly quick and easy to make and is an unusual and tasty way to eat an often maligned vegetable. Heat **2 tablespoons sunflower oil** in a large frying pan set over a medium heat. Add **1 teaspoon yellow mustard seeds** and fry until they begin to pop. Add **500g small cauliflower florets** and fry for 3-4 minutes, stirring occasionally. Add **1/2 teaspoon red chilli flakes** and **1/2 teaspoon ground turmeric**, and fry for a further 2-3 minutes or until the cauliflower is tender and can be easily pierced with a fork. Remove the pan from the heat and stir in **1/2 teaspoon toasted fenugreek seeds**, **1 teaspoon sea salt** and **1 tablespoon lemon juice**. Spoon into sterilised jars and seal. To make your sandwich, take **2 slices of granary bread** and spread with butter. Layer **25g Cheddar slices** over one of the slices, spread with 1 tablespoon of the pickle and top with the remaining slice of bread. Serves 1

LUNCH

FATOUSH SALAD WITH GRILLED HALLOUMI

This lunch hails from the eastern Mediterranean. Fatoush is made with the Lebanese/Syrian equivalent of croûtons – small pieces of toasted pitta bread, which soak up the juices of this hyper-fresh salad and provide its body. Squeaky grilled halloumi is the perfect accompaniment.

3 pitta breads
4-5 tablespoons olive oil
2 Little Gem lettuces, roughly shredded
1 medium size cucumber, peeled, deseeded and diced
6 spring onions, trimmed and sliced
200g baby plum or cherry tomatoes, halved

6 radishes, sliced
1 red pepper, deseeded and roughly chopped
1 green pepper, deseeded and roughly chopped
3 tablespoons freshly chopped flatleaf parsley
2 tablespoons freshly chopped coriander
juice of 1 lemon
1-2 teaspoons sumac
salt and freshly ground black pepper

SERVES 4

Preheat the grill. Toast the pitta breads on both sides until puffed up and starting to crisp. Split in half, brush with a little olive oil and toast the insides until lightly golden. Break into bite-size pieces and cool.

Tip all of the prepared vegetables into a bowl and gently mix with the chopped herbs.

In a small bowl mix together the lemon juice, remaining olive oil and season well with salt and freshly ground black pepper. Pour over the salad, sprinkle with the sumac and mix to combine Leave to one side for 30 minutes to let all of the flavours mingle and then serve with hummus (see page 23) and pan-fried halloumi.

SIDE

BAKED COURGETTES, FETA AND TOMATOES

Preheat the oven to 200°C/gas mark 6. Heat a griddle pan. Take **4 courgettes** and cut each in half lengthways. Brush with **olive oil** and cook them quickly for 2 minutes on the flesh side until lightly charred. Repeat the process with **3 halved tomatoe**s. Put the courgettes and tomatoes into a shallow ovenproof dish and season. Drizzle over **1 tablespoon balsamic vinegar**, a little **olive oil**, **150g diced feta**, a few sprigs of **lemon thyme** and **salt** and **freshly ground black pepper**. Cook in the oven for 20–30 minutes or until the courgettes are tender. Serve with some **fresh basil leaves**. Serves 4

DINNER

ASPARAGUS RISOTTO

SERVES 4

Morels are wild mushrooms with strange, pitted surfaces that make them look like little brains on stalks. They appear in the Spring and have a wonderful nutty flavour which infuses this delicate risotto. We wouldn't advise you to eat wild morels you think you've found unless you really know what you are doing but fortunately they are readily available in dried form.

6 morels, fresh or dried
250g thin asparagus, cut into 2.5cm pieces
25g unsalted butter
1 ½ tablespoons olive oil
1 red onion, finely chopped
300g Arborio rice
800ml vegetable stock, boiling

1 tablespoon fresh marjoram or oregano
(or 1 teaspoon dried)
2 tablespoons mascarpone
salt and freshly ground black pepper
freshly grated vegetarian Parmesan
(optional)

Soak fresh morels in salted water for 10 minutes and wash thoroughly. Pat dry and cut each into several pieces. If using dried morels, soak in hot water for 30 minutes before draining, drying and cutting up. Blanch the asparagus in boiling water for 1 minute, drain and set aside. Heat the butter and oil in a heavy-bottomed pan and sauté the onion and morels until soft. Stir in the rice and coat it well with the oil and butter. Pour in a cup of the stock and the marjoram and cook over a low heat, stirring frequently, until the liquid is absorbed. Add more cupfuls of stock one at a time and continue cooking until the rice is just tender and the consistency is creamy. Stir in the asparagus and the mascarpone and season well. Serve with Parmesan, if you wish.

DESSERT

RASPBERRY AND ALMOND TRAYBAKE

Preheat the oven to 180°C/gas mark 4. Grease a rectangular cake tin (about 31 x 17 x 3cm). Put **225g self-raising flour**, **75g ground almonds**, **200g diced butter** and **275g golden caster suga**r into a food-processor and whizz until the butter is evenly distributed — or rub together by hand in a large mixing bowl. Add **2 medium organic eggs** and the **finely grated zest of 2 oranges** and whizz quickly in the food-processor or mix with a wooden spoon. The mixture does not need to be very smooth. Spread the mixture over the base of the cake tin, then scatter **200g frozen raspberries** over the top. Bake in the oven for 45 minutes. Remove from the oven and scatter another **200g frozen raspberries** over the surface. Cook for a further 15 minutes, until firm to the touch. Cool in the tin and cut into squares. They will keep for up to two days in the fridge. Makes 16–24 slices

WEEK 13

BREAKFAST
SCONES

Preheat the oven to 200°C/gas mark 6. Grease a baking tray with oil or butter. Sift **125g wholemeal stoneground flour**, **125g self-raising flour**, **1 teaspoon baking powder** and **a good pinch of salt** into a bowl, and tip in any bran caught in the sieve. Add **75g of butter** (cut into small pieces) and rub it into the flour using your fingertips until the mixture looks like breadcrumbs. Mix in **about 60ml organic milk** to form a soft dough; don't make it too firm as the flour will continue to absorb moisture and firm up while you work. Turn the dough onto a floured surface and knead it lightly. Roll out the dough to a thickness of 1.5cm. Using a 5cm cutter, cut out 12 scones, and place on the baking tray. Bake for 15–20 minutes until golden and risen. Cool on a wire rack. Makes 12

PACKED LUNCH
BLUE CHEESE PATE

Hard boil **2 organic eggs** and separate the cooked egg yolks from the whites. Blend **250g vegetarian blue cheese of your choice** with the egg yolks and **50g unsalted butter**. Chop the egg whites finely and stir them and **2 tablespoons lightly toasted pine nuts** into the mixture. Transfer to a small dish and chill thoroughly. Serve with **bread**. Serves 2

LUNCH
WATERCRESS SOUP WITH TOASTED ALMONDS

SERVES 3

Watercress makes you feel alive. It is packed with freshness and iron and has more than enough flavour to carry a dish. Linda used to do a version of this soup, which is incredibly easy to make. Eating it will make you feel both virtuous and satisfied. The cream and garlic toasts add a touch of luxury, as do the flaked almonds, which are Stella's addition.

50g unsalted butter
2 medium onions, chopped
1 garlic clove, crushed
2 medium floury potatoes, peeled and diced
850ml vegetable stock
3 bunches watercress, roughly chopped
120ml single cream
salt and freshly ground black pepper
2–3 tablespoons crème fraîche, to serve
2 tablespoons toasted flaked almonds, to serve

FOR THE GARLIC TOASTS
6 thin slices of baguette, cut into long slices on the diagonal
2 tablespoons olive oil
1 rounded tablespoon freshly grated vegetarian Parmesan
1 fat garlic clove
1 tablespoon finely chopped parsley

Heat the butter in a large saucepan and lightly fry the onions and garlic for 2–3 minutes until tender but not coloured. Add the potatoes and sauté gently for a further 3 minutes. Add the vegetable stock, cover and simmer gently for 15 minutes or until the potatoes are tender.

Meanwhile, make the garlic toasts. Preheat the grill and toast the baguette slices on one side. Mix the olive oil, Parmesan, garlic and parsley together and spread over the untoasted side. Place back under the grill until golden and toasted.

Add the watercress to the pan, cook for 2–3 minutes, then pour the mixture into a liquidiser and blend until velvety smooth. Pour back into the pan, add the cream, season well and reheat gently. Serve in bowls with a swirl of crème fraîche, the garlicky toasts and a scattering of toasted flaked almonds.

SNACK

CHEESE AND ASPARAGUS CROQUETTES

Boil **500g potatoes**, drain, mash and place in a bowl. Steam **50g asparagus** until just tender, cut into thin slices and add to the potato. Beat in **2 organic egg yolks**, and season with **salt** and **freshly ground black pepper**. Cut **100g mozzarella** into cubes. Take a large spoonful of the potato mixture and mould round a teaspoonful of the cheese to form a sausage shape. Repeat until both mixtures have been used up. Lightly coat the croquettes in **plain flour**, then dip them first in **1 lightly beaten organic egg** and then **100g toasted breadcrumbs**. Half fill a deep saucepan with **vegetable oil**, heat to 170°C and deep fry the croquettes in small batches for 2–3 minutes until golden and crisp. Remove and drain on kitchen paper. Serves 4

DINNER

SICILIAN CAULIFLOWER PASTA

SERVES 4

Sicily was ruled by Arabs in the tenth and eleventh centuries and their culinary legacy lives on in the use of ingredients like saffron, raisins and pine nuts in the island's cooking. Here all three are combined with the humble cauliflower to create a memorable pasta dish.

a pinch of saffron threads
1 small-medium cauliflower, chopped
*   into small florets*
3 tablespoons olive oil
1 onion, finely chopped
2 fat garlic cloves, crushed
a pinch of crushed dried chilli
50g raisins
50g pine nuts

2 tablespoons sun-dried tomato paste
1 bay leaf
400g wholewheat mafalda corta
1 tablespoon lemon juice
2 rounded tablespoons freshly chopped
*   flatleaf parsley*
freshly grated vegetarian Parmesan, to serve
salt and freshly ground black pepper

Soak the saffron threads in 2 tablespoons boiling water and set aside.

Cook the cauliflower florets in a large pan of boiling salted water for about 4 minutes until tender. Scoop the cauliflower out of the pan, drain and set aside, and reserve the water.

Heat the olive oil in a large sauté pan, add the onion and cook over a medium heat until tender but not coloured. Add the garlic and chilli and cook for a further minute. Add the raisins and pine nuts to the pan and continue to cook until the pine nuts are toasted and lightly golden.

Add the cauliflower, steeped saffron, sun-dried tomato paste and bay leaf to the pan along with 150ml of the cauliflower cooking water. Season and cook over a low-medium heat for about 5 minutes, lightly mashing the cauliflower with the back of a wooden spoon to make a sauce and adding more water if necessary if it starts to look dry.

Meanwhile cook the mafalda corta in the cauliflower water according to the packet instructions. Drain, reserving 1 cupful of the water and tip the pasta into the sauté pan with the cauliflower sauce. Add the lemon juice, chopped parsley and stir to combine. Add some of the reserved water if needed. Serve with lots of freshly grated vegetarian Parmesan.

DESSERT

PEANUT BUTTER AND BANANA CUPCAKES

Preheat the oven to 180°C/gas mark 4. Line a 12-hole muffin tin with paper cases. In a large bowl, cream together **50g unsalted butter**, **100g smooth peanut butter** and **150g light soft brown sugar** for 3–5 minutes until pale and fluffy. Beat in **2 organic eggs** one at a time, whisking between each addition. Fold in **150g sifted plain flour** and **1 tablespoon baking powder** until you have a thick batter. Stir in **120ml soured cream**, then gently fold in **2 mashed medium ripe bananas**. Spoon the mixture into the muffin cases until two thirds full. Bake for 20–25 minutes until risen and the sponge bounces back when touched. Remove from the oven and leave to cool on a wire rack. For the frosting, place **75g cream cheese** and **75g smooth peanut butter** in a large mixing bowl and using a hand-held electric whisk, whisk until light and fluffy. Slowly add **300g icing sugar** one tablespoon at a time, whisking between each addition. The icing will be stiff to begin with, but don't be tempted to loosen it with any liquid, just continue whisking and it will soften up. Spoon the frosting into a piping bag fitted with a star nozzle. Pipe swirls of frosting over the cupcakes and sprinkle with **chopped peanuts** to decorate. Makes 12

SUMM

R

E

WEEK 01

BREAKFAST

FRUIT, SEED AND NUT MUESLI

Mix together **500g oat flakes, 250g barley flakes** and **25g each of sultanas, raisins, chopped dried apricots, sunflower seeds, chopped pecans** and **chopped brazil nuts**. To serve, add **organic milk** and drizzle with **honey**, or moisten with a splash of milk and stir in some **natural yogurt**. Keep in a sealed container. Makes 12 servings

---

PACKED LUNCH

MEXICAN BEAN SALAD

Warm **75g cooked black-eyed beans** in a pan and mix them with **3 tablespoons olive oil** and **1 tablespoon red wine vinegar**. Allow to cool then stir through **half a diced red pepper, 1 diced plum tomato, 1 crushed garlic clove, 1/2 finely sliced red onion** and **2 tablespoons freshly chopped flatleaf parsley**. Season to taste with **salt** and **freshly ground black pepper**. Serves 2

LUNCH

COURGETTE, POTATO AND DILL FRITATTA

A frittata is an Italian-style omelette, thicker than the standard kind in the UK. As with its famous Spanish cousin, it isn't folded but cooked in two stages: first 'bottom up' on the hob, then 'top down' under the grill. The second process creates a delectable savoury crust, as in the recipe below.

6 medium size new potatoes, scrubbed
1 large courgette, cut into 1cm slices
2 tablespoons olive oil
1 garlic clove, crushed
6 large organic eggs

1 rounded tablespoon freshly chopped dill
2 tablespoons freshly grated vegetarian Parmesan
1 teaspoon butter
salt and freshly ground pepper

SERVES 4

Cook the potatoes in boiling salted water for 20 minutes or until tender. Drain, allow to cool and then cut into slices.

Heat 1 tablespoon of the olive oil in a large frying pan and cook the courgette slices over a high heat until golden on both sides. Remove from the pan and cool. Add the remaining oil to the pan with the sliced potatoes and sauté until golden, then add the crushed garlic and cook for a further 30 seconds. Remove from the pan and cool.

Whisk the eggs together with the chopped dill and half of the vegetarian Parmesan and season with salt and freshly ground black pepper.

Preheat the grill. Melt the butter in a large 20cm frying pan and add the sautéed veggies in an even layer. Pour the cheesy egg mixture around the vegetables, scatter with the remaining Parmesan and cook over a low-medium heat for 3–4 minutes until the egg starts to set. Slide the pan under the grill and continue to cook until the top is set, golden and bubbling. Cool briefly and then cut into wedges to serve.

SNACK

SPINACH FILOS

Preheat the oven to 180°C/gas mark 4 and grease a baking tray. Wash **500g spinach leaves**, discard the stems, and cook the leaves in their own juice in a pan with the lid on until they wilt, then drain well and roughly chop. Mix with **75g mashed feta** (or cottage cheese), **a good pinch of nutmeg**, **1 organic egg** and season with **salt** and **freshly ground black pepper**. If using feta you may not need to add salt. Cut **125g filo pastry sheets** into rectangular strips about 7cm wide. Put the strips in a pile and cover with clingfilm to prevent them from drying out. Brush a strip of filo with **melted butter**, put 1 heaped teaspoon of filling at one end about 2cm from the edge and fold one corner up over it. Then fold again and again until the whole strip is folded into a small triangle (ensure you close any holes, as liquid from the filling can ooze out). Place close to each other on the baking tray and brush lightly with melted butter. Bake the filo parcels for 30 minutes or until crisp and golden. Serve hot. Makes about 15

DINNER

AUBERGINE PARMIGIANA

SERVES 4

With its tender aubergine and gooey mozzarella, this is deservedly a classic. Cooking with aubergines can seem daunting to Northern Europeans — they seem to absorb an impossible amount of olive oil if you fry them, for instance — but the Italians have got it down to a tee. The secret is to make sure you cook them right the way through.

5 tablespoons olive oil
2 garlic cloves, thinly sliced
2 x 400g can tomatoes
1 small bunch basil leaves, torn
1 teaspoon caster sugar
1 cinnamon stick

3 medium aubergines, cut lengthways into 0.5cm pieces
2 balls mozzarella, sliced
freshly grated vegetarian Parmesan
salt and freshly ground black pepper

Preheat the oven to 180°C/gas mark 4. Heat 2 tablespoons olive oil in a pan, add the garlic and fry gently for 2 minutes. Add the tomatoes and simmer for 15 minutes until thickened. Stir in the basil and season with salt and freshly ground black pepper, and the sugar.

Preheat a ridged griddle pan. Brush both sides of the aubergine slices with the remaining oil, season and griddle, turning a few times until completely tender (you could also do this in a non-stick frying pan). It's important to get the aubergines as tender as possible.

Put a few spoonfuls of the tomato and basil sauce in the bottom of a 26 x 20cm ovenproof dish, cover with the aubergine and mozzarella then repeat, ending with a thin layer of sauce (you'll have roughly 3-4 layers). Sprinkle with vegetarian Parmesan and bake for 30-40 minutes until bubbling and golden.

DESSERT

STRAWBERRIES WITH MASCARPONE AND CREAM

PINK

Hull **a 250g punnet of strawberries**. Mix together **1 tablespoon mascarpone**, **150ml whipping cream** and **¼ teaspoon vanilla extract** and **sugar to taste**. Scoop some over the strawberries and throw **a couple of blueberries** on top. Serves 2

WEEK 02

BREAKFAST

NECTARINE SMOOTHIE

Roughly chop **1 banana** and place in a blender. Add **100g nectarine flesh**, **50g porridge oats**, **100ml Greek yogurt**, **150ml organic whole milk**, **6 ice cubes** and **honey** to taste. Blend until smooth. Any ripe fruit, such as strawberries, raspberries, peaches or blueberries can be substituted for the nectarines, if you prefer. Serves 2

LUNCH

FRESH TOMATO AND BASIL SOUP

Heat **1 tablespoon olive oil** in a saucepan, add **1 large diced onion** and cook for 8–10 minutes until softened. Halve **375g ripe tomatoes** and add to the pan with the onion and cook for a further 5 minutes, breaking down with a spoon. Take another **375g tomatoes**, pierce each one and place in a bowl of boiling water for 20 seconds to remove the skins. Cut into chunks, removing the seeds, and set to one side. Place the onion mixture in a blender with **150ml vegetable stock** and blend until smooth. Pass through a sieve to remove the skin and pips and return to the pan with **1 litre of tomato juice**, **salt** and **freshly ground black pepper**, **a few shredded basil leaves** and the diced tomatoes. Heat through and serve sprinkled with **shredded basil leaves** and a swirl of **cream**, if desired. Serves 4

PACKED LUNCH

BROAD BEAN SALAD WITH CHEESE CHIPS

GIORGIO LOCATELLI

SERVES 4

This salad proves the rule that the simplest recipes are often the best. Aside from the vinaigrette, it only has four ingredients, but they complement each other so well that the whole is greater than the sum of the parts. Peeling the leathery skin of the broad beans may seem like hard work but releasing the delicate green nuggets within is worth the effort.

4 big handfuls of broad beans
120g pecorino, finely grated
4 handfuls of mixed leaves
3 tablespoons olive oil
1 tablespoon white wine vinegar
salt and freshly ground black pepper

TO SERVE
50g flour
50g vegetarian Parmesan, finely grated
100g pecorino, finely grated

Bring a large pan of salted water to the boil, put in the broad beans and blanch them for 2–3 minutes, then drain and refresh in iced water. Peel off the outer skins of the beans. If the beans differ strongly in size, cook them separately according to size.

To make the chips, mix the flour with the vegetarian Parmesan and the pecorino. Heat a couple of small non-stick pans and sprinkle a thin layer of the mixture all over the pan. Let it cook until it starts to turn golden. Turn the chips over and let them colour on the other side. Keep separate.

Whisk together the olive and white wine vinegar. Season the broad beans with salt and freshly ground black pepper, pour over the vinaigrette and add the pecorino. Lay the broad beans flat in the centre of the plate. Dress the mixed leaves and put on top of the broad beans. Serve with the pecorino chips.

SIDE
MEXICAN CORNBREAD

Preheat the oven to 180°C/gas mark 4. Lightly grease a 20cm round baking tin and dust with a little plain flour. Deseed **1 green chilli** and **1 red chilli** and chop finely. Trim and slice **6 spring onions**. Heat **a little olive oil** in a frying pan over a medium heat, add the spring onions and chillies and cook for a couple of minutes until soft but not coloured. Remove from the heat, tip into a bowl and add **340g can drained sweetcorn** and **2 tablespoons finely chopped coriander**. Beat **2 large organic eggs** together with **120ml of soured cream** and add to the sweetcorn mixture. Sift **175g polenta** and **2¹/₂ teaspoons baking powder** into the bowl, add **180g grated Cheddar** and season with **salt** and **freshly ground black pepper**. Pour into the prepared tin, spread level and scatter with another **40g grated Cheddar**. Bake on the middle shelf of the preheated oven for 35–40 minutes or until golden and well risen, and a skewer inserted into the middle of the cornbread comes out clean. Serves 4–6

DINNER

QUESADILLAS WITH AVOCADO, SOURED CREAM AND SALSA

SERVES 4

Quesadillas are the Mexican equivalent of toasted cheese sandwiches. They can be made with corn tortillas, which need to be softened before they are folded, but this recipe uses the soft flour kind, which are more pliable.

4 large flour tortillas
4 teaspoons olive oil
100g Cheddar, grated
50g chestnut mushrooms, thinly sliced
1 bunch spring onions, thinly sliced
4 tomatoes, skinned and chopped
2 ripe avocados, peeled and sliced
100ml soured cream

FOR THE SALSA
4 large tomatoes, deseeded and roughly chopped
2 spring onions, finely chopped
1 red chilli, deseeded and chopped
1 tablespoon white wine vinegar
3 tablespoons extra virgin olive oil
1 teaspoon caster sugar
1 tablespoon freshly chopped basil leaves

First make the salsa. Mix the tomatoes with the spring onions, chilli, white wine vinegar, extra virgin olive oil, caster sugar and basil. Chill until required.

Pour 1 teaspoon of the olive oil into a large heavy-bottomed frying pan set over a medium high heat, tipping the pan so the base becomes covered in oil. Take one of the tortillas and place in the pan. After 10 seconds, flip the tortilla over. Continue to flip the tortilla at 10-second intervals until air pockets begin to form within it.

Take a quarter of the cheese and sprinkle it over the tortilla, then add a quarter of the mushrooms, spring onions and tomatoes, taking care not to layer the ingredients too thickly.

Reduce the heat to medium low and cover the pan with a lid. If the quesadilla begins to smoke, remove from the heat. After a minute, check to see if the cheese is melted. If not, replaced the cover, and check again after 15 seconds. When the cheese is melted, carefully lift up one side of the quesadilla and fold it over as if making an omelette. Remove from the pan and keep warm. Repeat with the remaining tortillas. Serve with the avocado and soured cream.

DESSERT

MANGO LASSI

In a food-processor, whizz **600g natural yogurt**, **2 peeled and diced mangoes**, **3 tablespoons pomegranate seeds** and **1 tablespoon runny honey** until smooth. Pour into 4 glasses and serve immediately. Serves 4

WEEK 03

BREAKFAST

MELON AND STRAWBERRIES

Heat **250ml water** and add **2 teaspoons sugar** and simmer for 10 minutes. Strain and leave the syrup to cool. Add the chopped leaves from a **small bunch of mint**. Prepare **2 honeydew melons** by dicing into small pieces, mix together with **150g strawberries**, hulled and halved. Pour over the syrup mixture to coat the fruit. Serves 6

PACKED LUNCH

ASPARAGUS, EGG AND CRESS SANDWICH

TRISTAN WELCH

Cook **20 asparagus spears** in boiling salted water for 3½ minutes. Cut **8 thin croûtons** into large rectangles and dice **2 soft-boiled organic eggs**. Take 2 croûtons and arrange pieces of the egg, asparagus, some **mayonnaise** and a bit of **watercress** in the croûtons. Season with **salt** and **freshly ground black pepper**. Serves 4

LUNCH

YELLOW COURGETTE AND GARLIC BRUSCHETTA

SERVES 2

Bruschetta (see Spring, Week 4, Lunch) is a classic Italian starter, but it is also great as a light lunch. It is incredibly quick to prepare and very versatile — add or take away ingredients according to your preferences. A delicious way to eat courgettes when they are at their most plentiful.

2 yellow courgettes, cut into 5mm thick slices
3 tablespoons extra virgin olive oil
1 tablespoon balsamic vinegar
a pinch of sugar
4-6 slices stone-baked baguette
1 garlic clove
freshly grated vegetarian Parmesan, optional
salt and freshly ground black pepper

Place the slices of courgettes in a bowl. Whisk together the extra virgin olive oil, balsamic vinegar and sugar. Pour over the courgettes, season with salt and freshly ground pepper, stir, and set aside for 30 minutes.

Preheat a griddle to hot and grill the courgette slices for 3–4 minutes each side until nicely charred. Set aside.

Preheat the grill and toast the baguette slices until golden on both sides. Crush the garlic clove with a little salt to form a paste. While still hot, spread each slice with some of the garlic paste and drizzle with a little more olive oil. Top each slice with a spoonful of the courgettes, and, if you wish, grate over a little vegetarian Parmesan.

SNACK

CASSAVA CHIPS

Slice **1 cassava** very thinly and leave to dry. Heat some **groundnut or vegetable oil** (do not allow it to smoke) in a wok or a deep pan. Deep fry 1–3 slices at a time by immediately submerging each below the surface of the oil. Remove quickly from the heat and drain well on layers of paper towels. Season with **salt** and **freshly ground black pepper** and serve straight away. Serves 2

DINNER

PAPAYA SALAD

Papayas, or pawpaws as they are known in some parts of the world, are sweet, perfumed tropical fruits with deliciously soft flesh. This is an ideal dish for communal eating on a hot summer evening, with everyone tucking in using lettuce leaves as scoops.

SERVES 2

2 garlic cloves, peeled
3–4 small fresh red or green chillies, chopped
2 yard-long beans or 20 French beans, chopped into 5cm lengths
175g fresh papaya, peeled, deseeded and finely chopped
1 tomato, cut into wedges
1 tablespoon granulated sugar
2 tablespoons lime juice

TO SERVE
Little Gem lettuce leaves

Pound the garlic in a large mortar, then add the chillies and pound again. Add the beans, breaking them up slightly, then tip into a bowl. Add the papaya to the bowl then lightly mash together, and then stir in the tomato and lightly mash again.

Add the sugar and lime juice, stirring well, then turn into a serving dish. Serve with Little Gem lettuce leaves, which can be used as a scoop for the mixture.

DESSERT

PINEAPPLE FRITTERS

Peel, core and thickly slice **1 large pineapple**. Coat the pineapple slices in **caster sugar** and set aside for 30–40 minutes. Sift **250g self-raising flour** into a bowl, make a well in the centre and add **2 beaten organic eggs** and **380ml cold soda (or sparkling) water**. Stir until smooth and free from any lumps. Heat some oil to 180°C for deep-frying in a deep heavy-bottomed pan (or when a cube of bread sizzles and turns golden when dropped into it). Dip the pineapple slices into the batter, drain off the excess and lower into the hot oil using a slotted spoon. Cook until golden and crisp. Carefully remove the fritters from the oil with a slotted spoon and drain on kitchen paper. Sprinkle over a little caster sugar and serve hot. Serves 4

WEEK 04

BREAKFAST
PEACH AND MELON SALAD

A deliciously refreshing salad that will keep a day or so in the refrigerator. Peel and slice **3 ripe peaches** and place in a bowl. Halve **1 small charentais or honeydew melon** and scoop out the seeds. Cut the flesh into bite-size pieces and add to the bowl. Whisk together **2 tablespoons lemon juice, 2 tablespoons orange juice** and **2 tablespoons golden caster sugar.** Pour over the fruit and gently toss. Chill before serving. Serves 4

PACKED LUNCH
CARROT SOUP

We don't appreciate cold soups enough in Britain. This one is deliciously refreshing, with the sharpness of the grapefruit contrasting nicely with the sweetness of the carrots. The Gordal olives and hazelnuts give it a definite Spanish feel.

50g butter
500g carrots, peeled and sliced
1 garlic clove, peeled and crushed
750ml water
1 sprig fresh thyme leaves, freshly chopped
1 sprig rosemary leaves, freshly chopped
150ml organic milk

2 pink grapefruit, peeled and segmented, segments halved
1 handful green Gordal olives, stones removed, halved
1 handful hazelnuts, crushed and toasted
1 punnet fresh micro coriander cress
2 tablespoons hazelnut oil
salt and freshly ground black pepper

SERVES 4

Heat a large pan until hot, then add the butter, carrots and garlic and gently cook over a medium heat for 2–3 minutes. Add the water, thyme and rosemary and season with salt and freshly ground black pepper. Bring to a simmer, then cover with a lid and cook for 5–6 minutes, or until the carrots are tender.

Remove the pan from the heat and stir in the milk. Allow to cool slightly, then transfer the mixture to a blender and blend until smooth. Place in the fridge to chill for at least 30 minutes.

To serve, divide the soup among four serving bowls. Arrange the grapefruit segments, olives, nuts and coriander cress on top of the soup, then drizzle over the hazelnut oil.

LUNCH
AUBERGINES WITH TOMATOES AND CREME FRAICHE

Preheat the oven to 180ºC/gas mark 4. Cut **1.2-1.4kg aubergines** into slices 1cm wide. Lay on kitchen paper, sprinkle with salt and leave to rest for 30 minutes. Pat them dry and heat **6-8 tablespoons olive oil** in a shallow frying pan and cook on both sides until nicely browned. Drain on kitchen paper. Melt **30g unsalted butter** in a pan and add **750g roughly chopped tomatoes, 2 deseeded, roughly sliced red peppers** and **4 roughly chopped garlic cloves.** Cook over gentle heat for 15 minutes to soften. Boil **300ml good-quality crème fraîche**, stirring over a high heat and then reduce the heat to medium. Chop in some fresh herbs — **lemon thyme** and **parsley** and **tarragon** are particularly good. Throw in **2 tablespoons finely grated vegetarian Parmesan.** Assemble in a shallow baking dish, starting with a layer of aubergines, followed by one of the tomato/pepper sauce and continue, finishing with a layer of tomato/pepper sauce. Then pour over the reduced crème fraîche/herb mixture and finally sprinkle over another **2 tablespoons grated vegetarian Parmesan.** Bake for 25–30 minutes. Remove from the oven and leave to cool a little before serving. Good brown bread is a lovely accompaniment. Serves 4

SIDE

SUMMER COLESLAW

STELLA McCARTNEY

Peel and coarsely grate **2 medium-large carrots** into a large mixing bowl. Finely shred **1/2 small white cabbage** and **a handful of trimmed mangetout** and add to the bowl. Finely slice **6 spring onions** and **a handful of trimmed radishes**, and add along with **1 tablespoon poppy seeds**, **2 tablespoons roughly chopped toasted hazelnuts** and **2 tablespoons freshly chopped flatleaf parsley**. In a separate small bowl whisk together the **juice of 1/2 lemon** and **3 tablespoons hazelnut oil** and season well with **salt** and **freshly ground black pepper**. Pour over the coleslaw and gently mix together. Spoon the salad into a serving bowl and scatter over **mustard cress** to serve. Serves 4

DINNER

REFRIED BEAN TACOS

PAUL McCARTNEY

SERVES 4

Refried beans are essential to a good taco. You don't have to fry them twice — the name comes about because of a mistranslation of the Spanish name 'frijoles refritos'. The 're' bit doesn't mean 'again', it just means 'very'. Half the fun of eating tacos is making them — you filling the corn shells with trimmings to your taste.

1 medium onion, chopped
1 tablespoon olive oil
230g can refried beans
2 medium tomatoes, chopped
1–2 teaspoons hot chilli sauce (optional)
4 taco shells
40g Cheddar, grated
1 Little Gem lettuce, shredded
salt

TO SERVE
avocado, sliced
soured cream
a squeeze of lime and lemon juice

Gently fry the onion in the olive oil in a large frying pan for 4–5 minutes, stirring frequently until soft but not coloured. Stir in the refried beans. Add the chopped tomato and fry until heated through. Season with salt.

Warm the taco shells according to the instructions on the packet and half-fill with the refried bean mixture. Top with grated cheese and shredded lettuce, garnish with sliced avocado and soured cream. If you like your tacos spicy (which I don't!) add 1–2 teaspoons hot chilli sauce to the tomato mixture.

DESSERT

COURGETTE CAKES

FEARNE COTTON

Preheat the oven to 180°C/gas mark 4. Line a 12-hole muffin tin with paper cases. Coarsely grate **2 medium courgettes** into a bowl. If they seem watery, place in a clean cloth and wring out as much of the liquid as you can. Combine **2 large organic eggs**, **125ml vegetable oil** and **100g caster sugar** in a bowl. Sieve in **225g self-raising flour** and **1/2 teaspoon bicarbonate soda** and beat until well combined. Stir in the courgettes and **100g chopped toasted walnuts**. Pour into the paper cases and bake for 30 minutes until risen, golden and firm to the touch. Allow to cool. Make the frosting by beating together **200g cream cheese**, **100g icing sugar** and **a few drops of vanilla extract**. Spread the frosting on top of the cooled cakes and serve. Makes 12

WEEK 05

BREAKFAST

GRANOLA AND BERRIES

In summer, liven up your usual granola with a delicious combination of fresh and dried berries. Place **3 tablespoons granola** (shop bought is fine or see page 193) in a bowl. Add **1 tablespoon mixed dried cranberries and cherries**. Moisten with **2 tablespoons organic milk** and stir in **2 tablespoons natural yogurt**. Top with a handful of fresh berries of your choice — **strawberries, blueberries** or **raspberries** all taste wonderful. Serves 1

PACKED LUNCH

CANNELLINI BEAN AND ROSEMARY 'HUMMUS'

Put **400g cannellini beans** into a food-processor with the **juice of 1 lemon, 1 crushed garlic clove, 100ml natural yogurt** and **a handful of rosemary leaves** and whizz until smooth. Season with **salt** and **freshly ground black pepper** and serve with **sticks of carrot, celery and cucumber** for dipping. Serves 2

LUNCH

MOZZARELLA AND TOMATO SALAD

SERVES 4

This classic, Italian-inspired salad is the perfect al fresco lunch and showcases summer's sun-ripened tomato harvest. It can be put together in a matter of minutes.

250g buffalo mozzarella, thinly sliced
6 ripe tomatoes, finely chopped
50g black olives
3 tablespoons extra virgin olive oil
3 tablespoons white wine vinegar
1 teaspoon coarse-grain mustard
2 tablespoons freshly chopped oregano or
   basil
freshly ground black pepper

Put the mozzarella and tomatoes on a serving dish with the olives. Make a dressing by combining the extra virgin olive oil, white wine vinegar, coarse-grain mustard, oregano or basil and freshly ground black pepper. Shake the dressing well, pour over the salad and serve immediately.

SNACK

GREEN PEA CURRY

Put **4 finely chopped and deseeded fresh green chillies** and **a grated 1cm piece of ginger** in a mortar or strong bowl and crush to a paste with a pestle or the end of a rolling pin. Put **2 tablespoons vegetable oil**, **450ml water**, **a pinch of bicarbonate of soda** and the ginger and chilli paste in a saucepan. Add **salt** and **asafoetida powder** to taste, stir well and heat. When hot, add **750g fresh or frozen peas** and cook for 10 minutes until warmed through. The peas should not change colour. Remove from the heat and serve with **naan bread** and garnished with **coriander** and **coconut shavings**, if you wish. Serves 6

DINNER

LITTLE GEM, SOFT-BOILED EGG, ROAST TOMATOES, CAPERS AND PARMESAN DRESSING

With its croûtons, lettuce and vegetarian Parmesan, this flavour-packed dish is a relative of the Caesar salad (see Spring, Week 5, lunch). The salty, savoury capers do a similar job to the anchovies in non-vegetarian versions, while the peppery rocket (arugula), roast tomatoes and tangy dressing provide a symphony of complementary flavours. We defy anyone to eat this and say that vegetarian food is bland.

8–10 medium size tomatoes, halved
5 tablespoons olive oil
1 sprig thyme leaves
8 baby leeks, trimmed and finely sliced
4 slices sourdough or country bread
2 garlic cloves, crushed
2 tablespoons chopped flatleaf parsley
4 organic eggs
3 tablespoons extra virgin olive oil

1 tablespoon white wine vinegar
1 teaspoon Dijon mustard
2 teaspoons roughly chopped capers
4 Little Gem lettuce, leaves separated
1 bunch wild rocket
1 tablespoon finely snipped chives
vegetarian Parmesan shavings, to serve
salt and freshly ground black pepper

SERVES 4

Preheat the oven to 170°C/gas mark 3. Arrange the tomatoes on a small baking tray, cut-side uppermost, drizzle with 2–3 tablespoons of olive oil and season with salt and freshly ground black pepper. Scatter with the thyme leaves and cook on the middle shelf of the oven for around 20 minutes. Add the leeks to the tray and cook for a further 15 minutes until soft and starting to caramelise at the edges. Remove from the oven and leave to cool to room temperature.

Meanwhile, prepare the herby croûtons. Slice the bread into rough chunks and toss with 2 tablespoons of olive oil, the garlic and the chopped parsley and season well. Tip onto a baking tray and cook on the top shelf of the oven until golden and crisp. Soft boil the eggs in salted water, drain and refresh under cold running water.

To make the dressing tip the extra virgin olive oil, vinegar, mustard and capers into a jam jar, season, screw on the lid and give a good shake. Taste and adjust the seasoning if necessary.

To serve, arrange a pile of the Little Gem and wild rocket leaves on individual plates and tuck in the tomatoes and leeks. Quarter the soft-boiled eggs and divide between the plates, scatter over the chives and herby croûtons and drizzle over the dressing. Using a vegetable peeler shave some vegetarian Parmesan over the top of each salad and serve immediately.

DESSERT

SUPER SMOOTH RASPBERRY SORBET

Put **250g golden caster sugar** in a saucepan with **250ml water**, bring to a simmer and cook for 2 minutes. Allow to cool completely. Whizz **500g raspberries** in a food-processor then push through a fine nylon sieve. Stir in the cooled sugar syrup and **2 teaspoons balsamic vinegar**. Lightly whisk **1 organic egg white**, add it to the raspberry mixture then churn in an ice cream maker according to the manufacturer's instructions. Spoon into a freezer box and freeze until ready to serve. Serves 4

WEEK 06

BREAKFAST

YOGURT, BANANA AND RYE TOAST

A more substantial version of Greek yogurt and honey. Toast **1 slice of rye bread** and spread with **2 tablespoons Greek yogurt**. Layer with **1 sliced banana**, and drizzle with **2 teaspoons runny honey**. Serves 1

PACKED LUNCH

RATATOUILLE

Preheat the oven to 180°C/gas mark 4. Slice **½ aubergine, 1 courgette** and **½ red** and **½ yellow pepper** into wedges. Put the vegetables, **1 crushed garlic clove** and **4 quartered tomatoes** in a roasting dish. Drizzle with **olive oil**, season with **salt** and **freshly ground black pepper** and mix well. Bake in the oven for 30 minutes or until the vegetables are tender. Stir in some **fresh basil leaves**. Serves 2–3

LUNCH

FRENCH BEAN, ROQUEFORT AND WALNUT SALAD

SERVES 4

Roquefort is a 'blue' cheese matured in the caves of Mont Combalou in Southern France. Made from sheep's rather than cow's milk, it is similar to Stilton but creamier and sharper. Like its English cousin, it goes extremely well with walnuts.

300g French beans, topped and tailed
250g Roquefort
125g walnuts, toasted
1 small radicchio
1–2 red and white chicory

FOR THE DRESSING
3 tablespoons of extra virgin olive oil
1 tablespoon balsamic vinegar
1 garlic clove, crushed
salt and freshly ground black pepper

Wash the beans and steam them over a pan of boiling water until just crunchy. Keep warm. Crumble the Roquefort and lightly crush the walnuts. Wash the radicchio and chicory thoroughly and shake dry. Whisk together the remaining ingredients to make a dressing.

Arrange the leaves in a bowl, top with the beans, walnuts and cheese. Pour over the dressing.

SNACK

MELON GAZPACHO

Finely chop **1 small red onion** and deseed and dice **1 green pepper**, **1 small round melon** and **2 big beefsteak tomatoes**. Put the prepared fruit and vegetables in a large bowl, along with **1 tablespoon caster sugar**, **5 tablespoons extra virgin olive oil**, **3 tablespoons sherry vinegar** and **100g good crusty white bread, cut into chunks**. Give a good seasoning with **salt** and **freshly ground black pepper** and pour over **1 litre of water** and mix all gently together. Chill in the fridge for at least 3 hours and garnish with **a bunch of flatleaf parsley** just before serving. So refreshing! Serves 4

DINNER

AUBERGINE AND DRIED APRICOT PASTILLA

BRUNO LOUBET

SERVES 4

Reading the ingredients for this recipe, you might think you were about to make a dessert rather than a main course. That's because in Morocco, where this dish originates, the distinction is less clear than in most other places. A pastilla is a sweet-savoury pie, often containing pigeon. You'll find this vegetarian version a revelation.

4 medium aubergines, diced
160g dried apricots, diced
1 tiny drop almond extract
100ml olive oil
2 medium onions, finely chopped
6 garlic cloves, finely chopped
1 tablespoon chopped ginger
1 tablespoon ground cumin
4 tablespoons honey
5 tablespoons red wine vinegar

1 handful fresh coriander
1 handful fresh mint
zest of 1/2 lemon
36 squares filo pastry
125g melted butter
60g flaked almonds, toasted
40g icing sugar
1 tablespoon ground cinnamon
salt and freshly ground black pepper

Preheat the oven to 180°C/gas mark 4. Sprinkle the aubergines with salt and leave for 20 minutes before rinsing with cold water, making sure to squeeze the water out. Place the dried apricots in a pan, cover with water and add the almond extract. Bring to the boil then leave to rest for 5 minutes. Heat a frying pan on a low heat, add a film of olive oil and then add the onion. Stir occasionally until soft and golden brown, then add the garlic, ginger and cumin. Stir well and then set aside in a bowl.

In the same pan add some more olive oil and start to pan fry the aubergines in batches, until golden brown and soft. When all of the aubergines are cooked, add the onion, honey, vinegar and drained apricots. Cook slowly to stew for about 10 minutes (covered with a lid), then remove from the heat and add the herbs and lemon zest.

Brush the sheets of pastry with butter, then layer six sheets on top of each other. You should now have six pieces of pastry. Place one on a 10cm tartlet mould, push in and then fill two thirds with the aubergine mixture. Finish with toasted almonds. Close by folding over the pastry, then turn upside down and place on a baking tray. Brush the top with butter then bake for around 12 minutes, until golden and crisp. To serve, dust the top of the pastry lightly with icing sugar and a line of cinnamon.

DESSERT

REDCURRANT CHEESECAKE

Melt **75g butter** in a pan, add **250g crushed gingernut biscuits** and stir to combine. Press the biscuit mixture in an even layer over the base of a 20cm springform tin, then chill in until set, about 1 hour. Beat together **300g cream cheese**, **250g mascarpone**, **100g caster sugar** and the **grated zest and juice of 1 lemon** until smooth. Add **300ml double cream** and continue to beat until the mixture is well combined. Spoon over the biscuit base, smooth the top and chill for at least 2 hours or overnight. Place **200g redcurrants** and **1–2 tablespoons caster sugar** in a pan and heat gently. Simmer until soft, about 15 minutes. Strain into a bowl through a nylon sieve, taste for sweetness, adding more sugar if necessary, and chill. Top the cheesecake with a further **100g redcurrants**, and serve the purée on the side. Serves 6–8

WEEK 07

BREAKFAST

SUMMER BERRY MUFFINS

Preheat the oven to 180°C/gas mark 4. Line a muffin tin with 8 paper cases. Mix together **200g mixed summer berries**, such as strawberries, raspberries and blueberries. Hull the strawberries and roughly chop if using. Sift **300g plain flour, 2 teaspoons baking powder, 1/2 teaspoon bicarbonate of soda, 125g caster sugar** and **a pinch of salt** into a large mixing bowl. In a separate bowl mix together **100g melted unsalted butter** with **1 beaten organic egg, 250ml buttermilk** and **1 teaspoon vanilla extract**. Make a well in the middle of the dry ingredients, pour in the buttermilk mixture and add the mixed berries. Stir until just combined and divide between the muffin cases. Sprinkle the tops with **1 teaspoon soft light brown sugar** and bake on the middle shelf of the oven for 15–20 minutes until golden brown and well risen. Best served warm or at room temperature on the day of baking. Makes 8

PACKED LUNCH

CHICKPEAS WITH RED CHARD AND ASPARAGUS

In a large frying pan or wok heat **2 tablespoons olive oil** and fry **1 chopped red onion** and **1 deseeded and finely chopped red chilli** gently for 2–3 minutes until softened. Add **250ml white wine** and **1 tablespoon tomato purée** and cook until reduced by half. Add **200g finely shredded red Swiss chard**, a **410g can of drained chickpeas, 125g halved asparagus tips**, blanched and refreshed, and cook for a further 2–3 minutes. Transfer to a serving bowl and sprinkle with **a handful of freshly chopped parsley leaves**. Serves 2

LUNCH

MOZZARELLA PASTA

TWIGGY

SERVES 2

This quick and easy recipe is like the greatest hits of Italian cooking rolled into one dish.

175g penne rigate
400g can plum tomatoes
2 tablespoons olive oil
125g freshly grated vegetarian Parmesan
2 tablespoons freshly chopped basil leaves
150g mozzarella, diced
salt and freshly ground black pepper

Preheat the oven to 200°C/gas mark 6.

Cook the pasta in boiling water for 10 minutes until just tender. Meanwhile heat the tomatoes and oil in a pan, breaking down the tomatoes gently with a wooden spoon. Add half the Parmesan, basil and season to taste. Bring to the boil and remove from the heat

Drain the pasta and place in an ovenproof dish. Pour the sauce over the pasta and stir through the diced mozzarella. Sprinkle with the remaining Parmesan and place in the preheated oven for 10 minutes until the cheese is golden. Serve immediately.

SNACK

BAYD MAHSMI

Hard-boil **6 organic eggs** and, when cool enough to handle, shell the eggs and cut them in half. Remove the yolks into a small bowl, mash them with **2 tablespoons Greek yogurt, 1 small, grated onion, 1 pickled cucumber, grated** and season with **salt** and **freshly ground black pepper**. Gently fill the whites with the mixture and top each egg with **a stoned black olive.** Serves 4

DINNER

ROASTED VEGETABLE PIZZA

SERVES 4

Everyone loves a pizza but they don't always have to be topped with mozzarella. This one is made with Gruyère, which has a stronger taste that brings out the flavour of the roasted vegetables. Making it is easy – you don't have to swirl the dough around your knuckles like a theatrical Italian chef unless you can't resist it.

250g plain flour, plus extra for dusting
1/2 teaspoon salt
7g sachet fast action dried yeast
1 organic egg
1 small aubergine, cut into 1.5cm wedges
1 red, green and yellow pepper, each deseeded and cut into eighths
1 courgette, cut into 1cm pieces
3 medium mushrooms, halved
3 garlic cloves, halved lengthways

1 tablespoon fresh rosemary leaves, roughly chopped
3 tablespoons olive oil
flour, for dusting
3 tablespoons sun-dried tomato paste
1 tablespoon freshly chopped basil leaves
40g sun-dried tomatoes, roughly chopped
75g Gruyère, grated
salt and freshly ground black pepper

Preheat the oven to 200°C/gas mark 6. You will need a 28cm pizza tin or baking tray.

Sieve the flour and salt into a bowl and add the yeast. Beat the egg with a 100ml water. Add to the flour mixture to make a stiff dough, adding a little more water if necessary. Knead for 5 minutes for the dough to become smooth.

Leave the dough in a warm place to rise for 1 hour or until doubled in size.

Meanwhile, roast the vegetables and garlic cloves on a baking tray, sprinkled with the rosemary, olive oil, and salt and freshly ground black pepper, for 25–30 minutes until softened.

Roll out the dough, place in the tin, lightly dusted with flour, or on a baking tray and spread over the sun-dried tomato paste. Arrange the roasted vegetables on top. Sprinkle wth the basil leaves and sun-dried tomatoes, cover with the Gruyère cheese and bake for 25 minutes until the base is crispy and the cheese melted.

DESSERT

WATERMELON GRANITA

Place **625g watermelon** in a food-processor or liquidiser and blend to a smooth purée. Add **125g caster sugar, 600ml water** and **3 tablespoons lemon juice**, and process again. Press the mixture though a fine nylon sieve to remove the seeds. Pour into a suitable freezer container, cover with a lid and place in the freezer for 2 hours. Remove and stir so that the ice that has formed around the sides and base of the container is mixed into the unfrozen centre, then re-cover and return to the freezer for another hour until firm. Remove, mix thoroughly again and then re-freeze for a further hour. Serves 4

WEEK 08

BREAKFAST

MANGO AND LIME

Cut in half **3-4 ripe mangoes**. Peel them and cut the flesh into chunks of about 8cm. Sprinkle with the **juice and zest of 2 limes**. Very refreshing. Serves 4

PACKED LUNCH

TRICOLOR CIABATTA

Cut a **small ciabatta** in half and toast under the grill. Drizzle some **olive oil** over the toasted ciabatta and layer some **slices of tomato and avocado** over one half of the bread. Tear **half a mozzarella ball** over the top and season with some **salt** and **freshly ground black pepper** and then sprinkle over some **fresh basil leaves**. Place the other half of the ciabatta on top. Serves 1

LUNCH

STUFFED TOMATOES WITH GRUYERE

Shirley Conran once famously said that 'life's too short to stuff a mushroom'. Well it isn't too short to stuff a tomato with this light savoury filling. When you eat the result, you'll consider it time well spent.

8 large ripe tomatoes or 4 beef tomatoes
350g white breadcrumbs (made from day-old bread)
150ml organic milk
2 organic eggs, lightly beaten
2 garlic cloves, crushed
2 tablespoons freshly chopped basil leaves

2 tablespoons finely chopped fresh parsley
1 onion, finely chopped
2 tablespoons toasted breadcrumbs
5-6 tablespoons grated Gruyère
olive oil
salt and freshly ground black pepper

SERVES 4

Preheat the oven to 180°C/gas mark 4.

Remove a slice from the top of each tomato and scoop out the pulp. Season the insides of the tomatoes with salt and freshly ground black pepper and arrange in a greased baking dish.

To make the stuffing, combine the white breadcrumbs with the milk and eggs in a bowl and add the garlic, herbs and onion. Season with salt and freshly ground black pepper and fill the insides of the tomatoes. Sprinkle over the toasted breadcrumbs and Gruyère and drizzle over a little olive oil to prevent burning. Bake until the tomatoes are tender, about 30 minutes.

SIDE

BASIL-SCENTED BRAISED FENNEL

Heat **4 tablespoons of olive oil** in a large flameproof casserole dish. Add **3 large fennel bulbs**, trimmed and cut into 1cm thick wedges, and cook for 5–8 minutes until golden brown, turning carefully with the aid of a fork. Pour in **150ml vegetable stock**, cover, and simmer gently for 20 minutes until the fennel is tender. Add a **handful of basil leaves** and seasoning 1 minute before the end of the cooking time. Serves 4

DINNER

RISOTTO WITH ARTICHOKES

SERVES 4

Who'd have thought something so good could be made from the buds of a giant thistle? You need to use young globe artichokes for this recipe — older ones are delicious if you just nibble the tender bases of the leaves but the rest of them (apart from the soft hearts) can be unpalatably tough.

8 small globe artichokes, prepared and
    trimmed (chokes removed if at all prickly)
2 garlic cloves, finely chopped
2 tablespoons olive oil
1 litre vegetable stock
75g butter

1 medium red onion, very finely chopped
300g risotto rice
3–4 tablespoons extra dry white vermouth
75g freshly grated vegetarian Parmesan
sea salt and freshly ground black pepper

Cut the artichokes in half and slice as thinly as possible. Fry gently with the garlic in 1 tablespoon of the olive oil for 5 minutes, stirring continuously, then add 120ml water, salt and freshly ground black pepper and simmer until the water has evaporated. Set aside.

Heat the vegetable stock and check for seasoning. Melt half the butter in the remaining oil in a large heavy-bottomed saucepan and gently fry the onion until soft, about 10 minutes. Add the rice and, off the heat, stir for a minute until the rice becomes totally coated. Return to the heat, add 2 or so ladlefuls of hot stock or just enough to cover the rice, and simmer, stirring, until the rice has absorbed nearly all the liquid. Add more stock as the previous addition is absorbed. After about 15–20 minutes, nearly all the stock will have been absorbed by the rice; each grain will have a creamy coating, but will remain al dente. You may not need to add all of the stock.

Add the remaining butter in small pieces, then gently mix in the vermouth, vegetarian Parmesan and artichokes, being careful not to overstir.

DESSERT

FRUITY AMARETTI

Lightly crush **125g Amaretti biscuits** and place in the base of a serving dish or 4 individual dishes. Place **250g ricotta cheese**, **2 tablespoons fresh orange juice** and **2 teaspoons clear honey** in a food-processor or blender and blend until softened. Alternatively place the ingredients in a bowl and beat together well. Scatter **250g halved strawberries** over the Amaretti biscuits, then add a layer of **peach slices** and spoon over the cheese mixture. Place in the refrigerator to chill. The biscuits will remain crisp for a couple of hours. Serves 4

WEEK 09

BREAKFAST

GRILLED FIGS WITH RICOTTA

Preheat a grill. Cut **2 fresh figs** in half lengthways. Lightly grease a small baking tin. Place the figs, cut side up, in the tin and grill for 3–4 minutes until they begin to soften. Meanwhile, combine **2 tablespoons ricotta** with **1 teaspoon runny honey** and stir until smooth. Place the figs on a plate and spoon the ricotta mixture over the top. Serves 1

PACKED LUNCH

PEPPER POCKETS

JAMES TANNER

You ate tortillas back in week 2, in the form of quesadillas. Now we're going to show you how to make them yourself. It's easy and very satisfying but if you haven't the time you can always use ready-made tortillas for the recipe below. You will end up with neat savoury parcels that are equally good hot or cold.

FOR THE TORTILLAS
200g self-raising flour, sifted
a pinch of crushed sea salt
120ml boiling water
1 teaspoon olive oil, plus extra for brushing
sunflower oil

FOR THE FILLING
2 red peppers
1 tablespoon olive oil
200g fresh spinach, chopped
250g Emmental, cut into 1cm cubes
75g black Niçoise olives, stoned and chopped
freshly ground black pepper

Preheat the oven to 220°C/gas mark 7. Place the whole peppers on a roasting tray and roast for 25–30 minutes until the skins start to blacken. Remove from the oven, place in a plastic bag, seal and set aside for 5 minutes (to help loosen their skins). Reduce the oven to 180°C/gas mark 4.

For the tortillas, sift the flour into a mixing bowl with the crushed sea salt. Add the water and 1 teaspoon olive oil and mix with your hands to form a soft dough. Knead for 2 minutes on a lightly floured surface until smooth and elastic. Brush the top of the dough with olive oil, return to the bowl, cover with a clean tea towel and leave to rest for 10 minutes.

SERVES 4

For the filling, heat the tablespoon of olive oil in a wok or large non-stick frying pan. Add the spinach and stir fry over a medium heat for 4 minutes until wilted. Remove from the heat and drain in a sieve, squeezing out any excess moisture. Remove the peppers from the plastic bag. Skin, deseed and slice, then set aside.

Divide the dough into 8 pieces and roll into small balls in your hand. On a lightly floured surface roll each dough ball into a circle roughly 22cm in diameter. Repeat with the remaining dough to make 8 flour tortillas. Place the spinach in a large bowl. Add the sliced red pepper, Emmental and olives. Mix together and season with freshly ground black pepper. Divide the spinach mixture into 8 and spoon into the centre of the tortillas. Brush the edge of each tortilla with water and fold the edges up around the spinach filling to make a parcel.

Heat sunflower oil in a deep fryer. Add the tortilla pockets and deep fry for 2 minutes on each side. Transfer to a roasting tin and bake for 12–15 minutes until golden.

Remove from the oven and leave to stand for 2 minutes before serving or leave to cool completely.

LUNCH

GUACAMOLE

Halve, stone and peel **2 ripe avocados**. Put the avocado into a food-processor with **125g drained and chopped sun-dried tomatoes**, **1 garlic clove** and **1/2 teaspoon ground coriander**. Whizz the ingredients together until the avocados are well chopped but not smooth. Add **1–2 tablespoons of lime or lemon juice** to taste and stir in **1 tablespoon freshly chopped coriander**. Season with **salt** and **freshly ground pepper**. Serve with tortilla chips and salsa. Serves 2

SIDE

SALSA

Skin and deseed **4 large tomatoes**, and cut into rough dice. Slice **2 spring onions** very finely and mix with the tomatoes, **1 tablespoon white wine vinegar**, **3 tablespoons extra virgin olive oil**, **1 teaspoon caster sugar** and **1 tablepoon basil**. Chill well. Serve with tortilla chips. Serves 2

DINNER

LENTIL STEW WITH PAN-FRIED HALLOUMI AND POMEGRANATE

KEVIN SPACEY

SERVES 4

The pomegranate seeds in this dish not only provide jewel-like colour but also offer a contrasting burst of flavour and texture to the halloumi and lentils.

250g Puy lentils, washed
3 tablespoons olive oil
8 baby courgettes, sliced into 1cm pieces
1 large onion, chopped
2 cloves garlic, crushed
1/2 teaspoon ground cumin
pinch crushed dried chilli flakes
1 tablespoon tomato purèe
125ml dry white wine
300ml vegetable stock
227g can chopped tomatoes
1 bay leaf
100g sliced chard (or cavalo nero or spinach)
8 cherry tomatoes

1 tablespoon pomegranate molasses
salt and freshly ground black pepper

FOR THE MINT SALSA
3 tablespoons fresh mint, roughly chopped
2 tablespoons flatleaf parsley, roughly chopped
1 heaped teaspoon capers
3–4 tablespoons extra virgin olive oil
1 clove garlic, crushed
juice 1/2 lemon

TO SERVE
250g block halloumi, sliced

Cook the lentils in a pan of boiling water until only just tender and then drain.

Meanwhile heat the olive oil in a large pan set over a medium flame. Add the courgettes and cook until golden, remove from the pan and set aside. Add another tablespoon of olive oil to the pan and tip in the onion and cook until tender but not coloured. Add the crushed garlic, ground cumin and chilli flakes and cook for a further 30 seconds. Add the tomato purée, stir to combine, pour in the wine, vegetable stock and canned tomatoes. Pop in the bay leaf and bring to the boil. Reduce to a gentle simmer and cook for 20 minutes. Add the lentils, cover and cook for a further 10 minutes until softened. Add the courgettes, chard, cherry tomatoes and pomegranate molasses, cover and cook for a further 5 minutes.

Meanwhile prepare the mint salsa. Tip all of the ingredients into a food-processor and whizz until combined. Taste and add salt and freshly ground black pepper.

Heat a non-stick frying pan over a medium heat, add the sliced halloumi cheese and cook until golden brown on both sides. Spoon the lentils into bowls, top with hot halloumi and a good spoonful of mint salsa and serve.

DESSERT

BLACKCURRANT ICE CREAM

Wash **500g blackcurrants** then tip into a heavy-bottomed saucepan with **150g granulated sugar** and **3 tablespoons water**. Warm the pan over a low heat, stir until the blackcurrants are soft and the sugar has dissolved. Purée in a food-processor, sieve out the seeds and leave to cool. When ready to make the ice cream, stir in **600ml double cream** and **3 tablespoons Crème de Cassis**. Put into an ice cream machine and churn for 20–30 minutes. Makes 800–900ml ice cream

WEEK 10

BREAKFAST

BANANA AND HONEY MUFFINS

Preheat the oven to 180°C/gas mark 5. Line a 12-hole muffin tin with paper cases. Place **250g self-raising flour, 25g dark brown sugar, 50g melted butter** and **2 small mashed bananas** in a large bowl and mix them together. In a second bowl, whisk together **2 medium size organic eggs, 2 tablespoons clear honey** and **5 tablespoons organic milk** and beat into the other ingredients to form a mixture of soft dropping consistency. Divide the mixture between the cases, filling almost to the top. Bake for 15 minutes until risen and firm to the touch. Remove from the oven and transfer to a wire rack. To make the icing, mix together the **honey, icing sugar** and **lemon juice** and place a little on top of each muffin. Makes 12

PACKED LUNCH

FREGOLA SARDA PASTA WITH TOMATOES

Sardinian food is very trendy at the moment and a taste of this rustic dish should show you why. One of the island's signature cooking ingredients is fregola sarda, a kind of pasta consisting of tiny beads. It's like couscous but nuttier, as the grains are lightly toasted after they are formed.

300g cherry tomatoes, halved
3 garlic cloves, whole and unpeeled
1 teaspoon caster sugar
½ teaspoon dried oregano
5 tablespoons olive oil
200g fregola sarda pasta
2 tablespoons pine nuts, toasted

30g roughly chopped basil leaves
2 tablespoons freshly grated vegetarian Parmesan
100g stoned black olives, halved or roughly chopped
100g soft goat's cheese
salt and freshly ground black pepper

SERVES 4

Preheat the oven to 190°C /gas mark 5.

Tip the tomatoes and garlic into a small roasting tin. Scatter the tomatoes with a little sugar and the oregano, season with salt and freshly ground black pepper and drizzle with 2 tablespoons olive oil. Roast for about 25 minutes until soft and starting to caramelise at the edges.

Cook the fregola sarda in boiling salted water according to the packet instructions.

Meanwhile make a pesto using a pestle and mortar or in a small food-processor. Take the garlic from the roasting tin and squeeze the flesh from the skin and pound it together with the pine nuts. Add the basil and the remaining olive oil and pound again until finely chopped. Add the Parmesan, season with salt and freshly ground black pepper and mix again until amalgamated.

Tip the warm fregola sarda into a bowl, add the roasted tomatoes and black olives. Crumble over the goat's cheese and gently fold the pesto into the pasta. Serve warm or cold.

LUNCH

FRESH PEA AND BROAD BEAN OMELETTE

Heat the grill to medium. Boil **150g peas** and **150g broad beans** for 4 minutes until just tender, then drain well. Beat **8 large organic eggs** with **a splash of organic milk** and some **salt** and **freshly ground black pepper**. Stir the vegetables into the egg mixture along with **1–2 tablespoons lemon zest** and **1 crushed garlic clove**. Lightly **oil** an ovenproof shallow pan and place on the heat. Pour in the egg mix and gently cook for 8–10 minutes until there is just a little un-set mix on the surface. Place under the grill and cook until set. Serves 4

SNACK

JACKET CHIPS WITH TARTARE-STYLE SAUCE

Cut **1.5kg Maris Piper potatoes** into 1cm thick slices, then cut again to give long chips about 1cm thick and 7cm long. Blanch in boiling water for 3–4 minutes. Drain well on kitchen paper until dry to the touch. Heat enough **vegetable oil** for deep-fat frying to 190°C and cook the chips until golden brown and crispy. Drain well and sprinkle with **salt**. Keep hot. Make the sauce by mixing together **250ml mayonnaise**, **50g chopped capers** and **50g chopped gherkins**. Season to taste with **salt** and **freshly ground black pepper** and serve with the chips. Serves 4–6

DINNER

SALAD OF WILD RICE, CHARRED SWEETCORN, SPICED PECANS, AVOCADO AND FETA

ANNA HANSEN

SERVES 3–4

Wild rice has an earthy nutty taste which domesticated strains lack. It makes the perfect base for this inventive, flavour-packed dish. It's probably been quite a while since you last used icing sugar in a salad!

2 cobs of corn
2 tablespoons olive oil
150g wild rice
1 small cinnamon stick
1 red chilli, split lengthways
1 red onion, finely chopped
3 tablespoons good-quality red wine vinegar

¼ teaspoon sweet smoked paprika
100g pecan nuts
1 tablespoon icing sugar
1 teaspoon cumin seeds
½ tablespoon freshly chopped coriander
1 avocado, cut into pieces
small bunch of watercress, washed
100g marinated feta

Preheat the oven to 150°C/gas mark 2.

Cut the kernels off both cobs of corn. Put 1 tablespoon of the oil in a big pan, add the kernels and fry over a high heat until charred in places. Simmer the wild rice, cinnamon and chilli in plenty of water until tender but still al dente, and strain (check your packet of wild rice for timings, and taste for tenderness). Leave to cool.

Caramelise the red onion in a pan in the remaining oil until soft. Add the vinegar and paprika and continue to cook until the vinegar has evaporated, remove from the heat, allow to cool and add the corn. Toss the pecans with the icing sugar, cumin seeds, salt and 1 tablespoon water. Bake for 10 minutes or until golden (keep checking to make sure they don't scorch).

Mix the rice, sweetcorn and onion, coriander, avocado and watercress together. Crumble over the feta and pecans and serve.

DESSERT

PISTACHIO MERINGUES

Preheat the oven to 110°C/gas mark ¼. Line 2 large solid baking trays with baking parchment. Tip **4–5 large organic egg whites**, **300g caster sugar** and **a pinch of salt** into a medium size heatproof mixing bowl and whisk to combine. Set the bowl over a pan of simmering water but do not allow the bottom of the bowl to touch the water. Whisk constantly until the sugar has dissolved and the mixture has turned from opaque to white and is warm. Tip the mixture into the bowl of a free-standing electric mixer and whisk on high speed for about 5 minutes until very stiff, glossy, white and cold. Add **25g finely chopped pistachios** and fold in using a large metal spoon. Divide the meringue into 8 even size portions. Scatter another **25g pistachios** on top. Bake for 1–1¾ hours swapping the trays around halfway through. Remove from the oven and leave to cool on the baking trays. Place **500g halved strawberries** in a large bowl with **300g raspberries**, the **juice of ½ lemon** and **3 tablespoons caster sugar** and set aside for an hour or so to allow the juices to start to run. Whip **500ml double cream** and fold in **200ml of Greek yogurt**. Serve the meringues with a good spoonful of the cream mixture, the macerated berries and **a drizzle of passionfruit**. Serves 4

WEEK 11

BREAKFAST
OEUF EN COCOTTE

Preheat the oven to 180°C/gas mark 4. Lightly grease a ramekin dish or teacup with **butter**. Crack in **1 organic egg** and pour over **1 tablespoon double cream**. Place in the oven and bake for 10 minutes or until the white of the egg is cooked through but not hard. Serve with **toast soldiers**. You can also add a **sprig of fresh thyme** or grate over some **Gruyère** before baking. Serves 1

PACKED LUNCH
GREEK SALAD

In a shallow bowl, arrange **300g sliced beefsteak tomatoes** and **1 finely sliced shallot**. Pour over several glugs of extra virgin olive oil. Scatter over **½ cucumber, peeled and diced, 100g black olives, 125g cubed feta, a handful of freshly chopped flatleaf parsley** and **leaves from 2 sprigs of oregano**, season generously with **salt** and **freshly ground black pepper** and serve with **warmed pitta bread**. Serves 4

LUNCH
STILTON PATE WITH MELBA TOAST AND CHERRY TOMATOES

ANDREW MAXWELL

SERVES 4

This is a very adult recipe. The pungency of the Stilton is diluted by the sweetness of the cream cheese, and the splash of brandy adds a touch of luxury. 'Nuking' the accompanying cherry tomatoes in the way described concentrates the flavour and slightly caramelises them.

100g Stilton
275g cream cheese
25–50ml double cream
½ tablespoon brandy
250g vine ripened cherry tomatoes

olive oil
balsamic vinegar
8 wafer-thin slices white bread
freshly ground black pepper

Preheat the oven to 220°C/gas mark 7.

Remove the rind from the Stilton. Place the Stilton in a food-processor and blend until smooth. With the motor running, add half the cream cheese, then the brandy very slowly. Do not overmix. Add the remaining cream cheese and sufficient double cream to give the required consistency. Season with black pepper. Place in a serving dish and smooth the surface.

Drizzle the cherry tomatoes with olive oil and balsamic vinegar and roast in the oven for 4 minutes, until the skin is just peeling off.

For the melba toast, turn the oven down to 160°C/gas mark 3, and remove the crusts of the bread and cut each slice diagonally. Place on a baking tray and bake in the oven until crisp and golden brown.

SIDE
WATERCRESS AND LETTUCE SALAD

Wash and trim **1 bunch watercress** and **1 large lettuce** and leave to drain. Make a dressing by mixing together **4 tablespoons olive oil, 2 tablespoons vinegar or lemon juice, salt** and **freshly ground black pepper, 1 tablespoon chopped onion, 1 crushed garlic clove** and **1 teaspoon mild mustard**. Coarsely chop the drained watercress and lettuce, place in a salad bowl and add the dressing. Serves 4

DINNER

PAELLA VERDURAS

JOSÉ PIZARRO

This recipe showcases summer vegetables like courgettes and fresh peas. Sweet pimentón (ground red pepper) and saffron are essential to any authentic paella. The latter is made from the stamens of crocuses – there are only three per plant, which explains why it's so expensive. Fortunately, you only need to use a tiny quantity.

½ teaspoon saffron strands
1 litre vegetable stock
240g shelled broad beans
100g fine green beans, topped and tailed and halved
100g fine asparagus, cut into 5cm lengths
3 tablespoons extra virgin olive oil
200g small courgettes, cut into thick slices
1 medium onion, finely chopped
1 large red pepper, deseeded and chopped into 1cm pieces
1 large green pepper, deseeded and chopped into 1cm pieces

3 garlic cloves, finely chopped
1 teaspoon sweet pimentón
200g tomatoes, fresh or from a can, skinned and chopped
400g short grain paella rice, such as Calasparra or Bomba
2 tablespoons freshly chopped flatleaf parsley
100g shelled peas
280g jar chargrilled artichokes in olive oil, drained
fine sea salt and freshly ground black pepper

SERVES 6

Shake the saffron strands around in a slightly hot frying pan for a few seconds until dry but not coloured, then tip into a small mortar or coffee cup and grind to a powder with the pestle or a wooden spoon. Add a splash of the stock and set aside.

Bring a pan of salted water to the boil. Drop in the broad beans, bring back to the boil and cook for 2 minutes. Lift out with a slotted spoon into a colander, leave to drain, then tip into a bowl. Bring the pan of water back to the boil, add the green beans and cook for 3 minutes. Remove with the slotted spoon to the colander and refresh under cold water. Tip onto a plate. Bring the water back to the boil once more, add the asparagus, bring back to the boil, drain and refresh under cold water. Pop the broad beans out of their skins and add to the plate of green beans with the asparagus.

Heat 2 tablespoons of the olive oil in a large non-stick frying pan or shallow flameproof casserole dish over a medium-high heat. Add the courgettes and fry them for 2–3 minutes until a light golden brown. Lift out onto a plate.

Add the remaining tablespoon of oil and the onion to the pan and fry gently for 5 minutes. Add the red and green pepper and continue frying until the onion is soft and lightly golden. Stir in the garlic and pimentón and fry for 1 minute more. Add the tomatoes and fry for 2–3 minutes until softened, then stir in the rest of the stock, the saffron mixture and some seasoning to taste and bring to the boil. Sprinkle in the rice and the parsley, stir lightly to evenly distribute the rice around the pan, then scatter over the cooked beans, asparagus, courgettes, peas and artichokes and shake the pan gently so that they all bed down slightly into the rice. Lower the heat and leave to simmer vigorously for 6 minutes, then lower the heat again and leave to simmer gently for a further 14 minutes, until all the liquid has been absorbed and the rice is tender, but still with a little bit of a bite to it. Remove the pan from the heat, cover with a large lid or clean tea towel and leave to rest for 5 minutes before serving.

DESSERT

GRILLED PEACHES WITH GREEK YOGURT

Preheat the oven to 200°C/gas mark 6. Spray **oil** on the bottom of a griddle pan or frying pan, heat, then add **4 halved and stoned peaches** cut-side down and cook for 5 minutes. Set the peach halves cut-side up in a roasting tin, pour **120ml orange juice** around them and drizzle with **1–2 tablespoons runny honey**. Roast for 10–15 minutes, depending on their ripeness. Place the peach halves into individual warmed bowls cut-side up, spoon on a **dollop of Greek yogurt** and scatter with **pistachio nuts**. Serves 4

WEEK 12

BREAKFAST

APRICOT AND OAT FINGERS

Preheat the oven to 190°C/gas mark 5. Grease and line a baking tin. Place **250g chopped dried apricots** and **3 tablespoons apple juice** in the small saucepan and simmer over a low heat for 5 minutes until soft. Place **175ml sunflower oil** and **4 tablespoons clear honey** in a medium saucepan and stir over a low heat until evenly blended. Add **175g porridge oats**, **150g plain flour** and **50g walnuts** and mix together thoroughly. Put half the mixture into the baking tin and press down firmly with the back of the wooden spoon. Cover with the apricot mixture, then sprinkle over the remaining oat mixture and press down firmly. Bake for 35 minutes until golden brown. Remove from the oven and leave to cool for 5 minutes, then cut into 14 fingers. Allow to cool completely before removing from the tin. Makes 14 pieces

---

PACKED LUNCH

GREEN CLUB SANDWICH

Toast **3 slices wholegrain or rye bread** and slice **1 small avocado**. Spread **3 tablespoons hummus** (shop-bought or see page 23) evenly over one side of each slice of toast. Lay half the avocado, some **rocket leaves** and **alfafa sprouts** over the hummus. Season with **freshly ground black pepper**, then cover with another slice of toast. Pile on the rest of the avocado, some more rocket and alfafa sprouts, season again and top with the third slice of toast. Serves 1

LUNCH

ORANGE MARINATED TOFU SKEWERS

PAMELA ANDERSON

SERVES 4

Tofu is great at absorbing flavours, in this case of a zesty citrus marinade. The only thing that's remotely difficult about this recipe is remembering to start marinating the skewers four hours before cooking them. Here, they're grilled but you could easily barbecue them.

FOR THE SKEWERS
*700g firm tofu, drained and cut into
   2.5cm cubes*
2 large onions, cut into 2.5cm pieces
*1 red pepper, deseeded and cut into
   2.5cm pieces*
*1 green pepper, deseeded and cut into
   2.5cm pieces*
*1 yellow pepper, deseeded and cut into
   2.5cm pieces*
450g whole cherry tomatoes
150-175g fresh orange pieces, to garnish

FOR THE MARINADE
225ml orange juice
55ml lemon juice
1 teaspoon chopped garlic
1¹/2 teaspoons whole black peppercorns
2 teaspoons fresh thyme leaves
zest of 1 orange
500ml olive oil

10 bamboo skewers

Combine all the ingredients for the marinade, except the oil, in a food-processor and blend for 15 seconds. While the machine is running, slowly add the oil until blended.

Thread the tofu, onions, peppers, and tomatoes onto the skewers. Place in a shallow dish and pour the marinade over the tofu and vegetables. Leave to marinate for 4 hours. Remove the skewers from the marinade and either griddle over a medium flame for about 4 minutes on each side or place under a grill, until the veggies are lightly cooked and have grill marks. Serve with the orange pieces.

SIDE

POTATO AND GRUYERE FOCACCIA

NICK MALGIERI

Make the dough by mixing **585g unbleached plain flour or bread flour** and **2 teaspoons salt**. Set aside. In a large mixing bowl, whisk a **7g sachet fast action dried yeast** into lukewarm **420ml tap water**. Wait 2 minutes and whisk again to make sure the yeast is completely dissolved. Whisk in **60ml olive oil**. Use a large rubber spatula to smoothly stir half the flour mixture into the liquid. Stir in the dough mixture, using the spatula to dig up any unmoistened flour from the bottom of the bowl. Use the spatula to beat the dough vigorously for about 15 seconds. Cover the bowl with clingfilm and let the dough rise until it has doubled in size, about 1 hour. Scrape the dough into a tin, being careful not to fold the dough over on itself. Reach under it and flip it over — now the top is coated with oil. Use the palms of your hand to press the dough into the tin. If it resists, cover, and let rest for 10 minutes, then press again to cover the entire base of the tin. Cover with clingfilm and let rise until puffy, about 30 minutes. Set a rack on the lowest level of the oven and preheat to 230°C/gas mark 8. Peel and thinly slice **2 medium waxy potatoes** and add them to a saucepan, cover with water and bring to the boil over a medium heat. Drain, rinse and set aside in a colander. Once the focaccia is risen, use your index finger to dimple the top all over at 2.5cm intervals. Cover with the potato slices. Season with a little **salt and freshly ground black pepper** and evenly scatter over **55g coarsely grated Gruyère**. Drizzle with **2 tablespoons olive oil**. Place the focaccia in the oven and reduce the temperature to 220°C/gas mark 7. Bake until the dough is firm and the topping is golden, about 30 minutes. About halfway through, use a wide palette knife to lift the corner of the focaccia to check that the base is starting to colour. If it is colouring too quickly, slide another tin under the tin the focaccia is in to insulate it. Slide the baked focaccia to a rack to cool so that the base doesn't become damp. Makes approximately 12 squares

DINNER

WARM HALLOUMI, APPLE AND RADISH SALAD

SERVES 4

The first word that comes to mind to describe this salad is 'crisp'. The contrast to the crunchiness of the apple and lettuce is provided by the fried halloumi, which is so dense it's almost meaty. The red chilli adds a bit of fire.

3 eating apples, cored and finely sliced
2 tablespoons lemon juice
3 Little Gem lettuces, leaves separated
250g radishes, trimmed and sliced
100g walnuts, toasted and roughly chopped
4 tablespoons olive oil

1 tablespoon wholegrain mustard
2 tablespoons runny honey
1 red chilli, deseeded and finely chopped
2 x 250g packet halloumi, each block cut into 4 slices

Place the apple slices in a bowl and toss in a tablespoon of the lemon juice to prevent them browning. Arrange the lettuce leaves on a platter. Scatter over the apples, radishes and walnuts.

Whisk together 3 tablespoons of the olive oil with the remaining lemon juice, mustard and honey and drizzle over the lettuce, apple and radishes.

Add the remaining tablespoon of olive oil to a large non-stick frying pan set over a medium heat and stir in the chilli. Add the halloumi slices and fry for 2–3 minutes on each side until the cheese is golden. You will need to do this in batches. Lay the hot halloumi over the salad and serve.

DESSERT

PAVLOVA WITH RASPBERRIES

Preheat the oven to 180°C/gas mark 4. Mark out a 20cm diameter circle on a sheet of baking parchment and place on a baking tray. Whisk **3 organic egg whites** with **150g caster sugar**, adding the sugar a tablespoon at a time, until the egg whites are glossy and form stiff peaks. Whisk in **1 level teaspoon cornflour** and **1 teaspoon white wine vinegar**. Spoon the mixture onto the baking parchment and shape to the circle, making a slight well in the centre so the edges are raised. Place in the oven and immediately reduce the heat to 120°C/gas mark ½. Bake for 1½ hours, then turn off the oven and leave the pavlova inside to cool completely. When ready to serve, whisk **300ml double cream** and spoon onto the pavlova. Top with **500g sliced raspberries** and dust with **a little icing sugar**. Serves 4

WEEK 13

BREAKFAST
BANANA YOGURT POT

Dollop about **1 tablespoon thick Greek yogurt** into the bottom of a small glass or bowl. Chop **1 banana** and add a layer of banana slices over the yogurt, then top with another layer of yogurt. Repeat the layers until the glass or bowl is full. Drizzle over some **honey** and scatter over some **granola** (see page 193), if you wish. Serves 1

PACKED LUNCH
GRILLED VEGETABLE BLOOMER

Preheat the grill. Cut **3 red peppers** in half, deseed, and place, cut-side down, on a baking tray. Place under the grill and char until the skins are blackened. Put the peppers in a plastic bag, seal and leave to cool. When cool enough to handle, remove the skins, cut into strips, drizzle with **1 tablespoon olive oil** and set aside. Slice **1 aubergine** into rounds about 5mm thick, and place on another baking tray. Add **2 thinly sliced red onions**. Drizzle with **2 tablespoons olive oil**, season with **salt** and **freshly ground black pepper**, and grill, turning occasionally, until nicely charred at the edges. Cut **a small bloomer loaf** almost in half lengthways (leaving a 'hinge') and carefully hollow out most of the bread, so you are left with a shell that has edges about 1cm thick. Spread the insides with a thin layer of **pesto sauce**, and add the peppers in a layer, followed by the aubergine and onion mixture. Close, cut into thick slices and wrap tightly with clingfilm until ready to eat. Serves 2

LUNCH
PANZANELLA

This classic Florentine salad of bread and tomatoes is ideal for a summer lunch. Until the twentieth century the salad was based on onions rather than tomatoes, but its evolution takes advantage of tomatoes when they're at their best.

1/2 loaf ciabatta
6 tablespoons extra virgin olive oil
2 garlic cloves, 1 peeled, 1 crushed
1/2 teaspoon dried oregano
2 tablespoons good-quality red wine vinegar
2 tablespoons freshly chopped flatleaf parsley
1 tablespoon baby capers, drained

6 plum tomatoes, roughly chopped
1 small red onion, finely sliced
1/2 cucumber, deseeded and cut into chunks
2 celery stalks, finely sliced
12 fresh basil leaves, ripped
50g stoned black olives, halved
salt and freshly ground black pepper

SERVES 4

Cut the ciabatta in half and brush the cut sides with a little extra virgin olive oil. Heat a ridged grill pan or normal grill and toast the ciabatta until crisp and golden. Rub the peeled garlic clove over the cut sides of the bread, tear the bread into rough chunks and set aside.

In a small bowl whisk together 5 tablespoons extra virgin olive oil, the crushed garlic clove and the red wine vinegar. Season well with salt and freshly ground black pepper and add the freshly chopped flatleaf parsley.

In a large bowl, mix together the bread and baby capers, plum tomatoes, sliced onion, cucumber, sliced celery, basil leaves, and black olives, and toss with the dressing. Season to taste.

SNACK

MACERATED STRAWBERRIES WITH MASCARPONE ON RYE

Hull and halve **250g strawberries** and place in a bowl. Pour over **2 teaspoons balsamic vinegar** and **1 tablespoon caster sugar**, season lightly with **freshly ground black pepper**, stir gently and leave to macerate for 1 hour. Toast **4 slices rye bread** and spread each with **1 teaspoon creamy mascarpone**. Top with a spoonful of macerated strawberries. Serves 4

DINNER

FETA AND COUSCOUS SALAD WITH POMEGRANATE

SERVES 4

Continuing with the hot weather theme, this is a dish you can imagine eating in Iran or Morocco in summer. It is filled with cooling ingredients like couscous, feta and mint, and the pomegranate seeds pop delightfully when you bite into them.

200g couscous
200g feta, roughly crumbled
35g shelled pistachios
150g pack pomegranate seeds
2 tablespoons freshly chopped mint

juice 1 orange
2 tablespoons white wine vinegar
2 tablespoons olive oil
salt and freshly ground black pepper

Place the couscous in a shallow bowl, then pour over 200ml boiling water. Cover the bowl with clingfilm, then leave for 5 minutes until the couscous has swelled up and absorbed all of the water. Ruffle with a fork to separate the grains, then stir through feta, pistachios, pomegranate seeds and mint.

Make a dressing by mixing together the orange juice, white wine vinegar and olive oil, then stir into the couscous. Season well with salt and freshly ground black pepper and serve.

DESSERT

TIRAMISU

Mix together **175ml strong black coffee**, **3 tablespoons Marsala or sherry** and **3 tablespoons brandy**. Place **4 trifle sponges** in a serving dish and pour over half the coffee mixture. Mix together **250g mascarpone**, **300ml double cream** and **4 level tablespoons icing sugar**. Spoon half over the sponges. Place **4 trifle sponges** on top, and pour over the remaining coffee mixture. Smooth the surface. Sieve **25g cocoa powder** over the top and chill for at least 2-3 hours before serving. Serves 4-6

U

AU T

U

T

LMN

WEEK 01

BREAKFAST

TOASTED RYE BREAD WITH CINNAMON HONEY BUTTER

Beat together **100g softened unsalted butter, 2 tablespoons runny honey** and **¼ teaspoon ground cinnamon** until light and fluffy. Chill in the refrigerator until set. Toast **4 slices of rye bread** in a toaster or under the grill, then spread with the cinnamon butter. Serves 2

PACKED LUNCH

EASY SPICED DHAL WITH POPPADOMS

Place a saucepan over a moderate heat and add **1 tablespoon olive oil**. Fry **1 finely chopped small onion, 1 finely chopped garlic clove, 2 peeled and finely chopped 2.5cm pieces of ginger** and **1 deseeded and finely chopped bird's eye chilli** for 2 minutes. Add **250g yellow split peas** and **600ml vegetable stock**. Bring to the boil, reduce the heat and cook for 40 minutes until the split peas are tender. Stir occasionally, particularly towards the end of the cooking time. Remove from the heat, add **salt** and **freshly ground black pepper** to taste and stir in **20g roughly chopped coriander.** Serve with **mini poppadoms**, if you wish. Serves 4–6

LUNCH

FIG AND GOAT'S CHEESE SALAD

STELLA McCARTNEY

SERVES 2

Luscious figs are married with the fresh tartness of goat's cheese in this recipe. Putting them on the griddle for a couple of minutes helps bring out their delicate flavour.

3 tablespoons olive oil
1 tablespoon balsamic vinegar
4 ripe figs, halved
olive oil, for brushing
100g goat's cheese, roughly sliced
2 handfuls of watercress, stems removed
salt and freshly ground black pepper

Whisk together the olive oil and balsamic vinegar and season with salt and freshly ground black pepper.

Heat a griddle pan until very hot. Brush the figs with a little olive oil. Put them cut-side down on the griddle pan and cook for 2–3 minutes. Remove carefully.

Arrange the figs, cheese and watercress on 2 plates. Drizzle with the dressing and serve.

SIDE
STIR-FRIED KALE

Thoroughly wash and dry **750g young kale** in a salad spinner. Chop it roughly. Pour **3 tablespoons peanut or olive oil** in a wok or heavy frying pan over a high heat and, when the oil is steaming, toss in the kale and cook for 3 minutes, stirring constantly. Season and add **lemon juice** and shavings of **lemon zest** for decoration, if you wish. Serve piping hot. Serves 4

DINNER

AUBERGINE CASSEROLE WITH POMEGRANATE

MAGGIE BEER

SERVES 3-4

Verjuice, which is made from unripe grapes, was an important cooking ingredient in medieval times. It has recently been re-popularised by Australian chef Maggie Beer. Being acidic, it can be used in much the same way as vinegar or lemon juice, for instance in salad dressings or marinades, but it has a mellower, fruitier flavour.

200g organic lentils
160ml extra virgin olive oil
3 medium aubergines, sliced
1 large onion, roughly diced
5 garlic cloves, finely chopped
3 tomatoes, roughly chopped
125ml verjuice
70g pomegranate molasses

2 tablespoons rinsed and finely chopped preserved lemons
3 tablespoons roughly chopped flatleaf parsley leaves
3 tablespoons roughly chopped mint leaves
400g quark
salt and freshly ground black pepper

Preheat the oven to 150°C/gas mark 2.

Place the lentils and 1.5 litres water in a saucepan, bring to a simmer and cook for 15 minutes. Drain and set aside.

Meanwhile, place a heavy-bottomed casserole dish over a high heat, add 3 tablespoons olive oil and fry the aubergine in batches until golden. Remove and set aside. Add the onion and cook for 10 minutes or until golden brown, stirring occasionally. Add the garlic, and a good pinch of salt and cook, stirring every now and then to prevent the onion from burning, for 3-4 minutes or until the onions are a golden brown colour.

Then add the tomatoes with 1 tablespoon olive oil and bring the mixture back to temperature. Pour in the verjuice and cook, stirring, for 1 minute until the liquid has reduced by two-thirds, then remove from the heat and set aside.

Add half of the aubergine slices, then sprinkle over half of the lentils, then add the rest of the aubergine and top with the rest of the lentils. Pour over the remaining olive oil and the pomegranate molasses. Cover and place in the oven to cook for 1 hour, then stir through the preserved lemons. Return to the oven for another 45 minutes–1 hour or until the aubergine is cooked through. Check for seasoning and serve warm with the parsley and mint stirred through. Serve on individual plates, top with quark and drizzle with a last dash of olive oil.

DESSERT

GLUTEN-FREE CRANBERRY POLENTA CAKE

Preheat the oven to 180°C/gas mark 4. Grease a 20cm springform cake tin. Place **125g polenta**, **250g all-purpose gluten-free flour**, **1 heaped teaspoon baking powder** and **150g golden caster sugar** in a food-processor with the **grated zest of 1 orange**, and process to combine. Add **150g diced unsalted butter** and process until the mixture resembles fine breadcrumbs. Combine **1 tablespoon orange juice**, **1 beaten organic egg** and **1 tablespoon olive oil** and, with the motor running, slowly pour into the processor through the feeder. Once combined, stop the machine and press two thirds of the dough into the cake tin. Combine **250g frozen cranberries**, **50g demerara sugar** and **2 teaspoons polenta** and pile into the base, leaving a border of about 1cm around the edge. Crumble over the remaining dough and cook in the oven for 45–50 minutes until golden brown. Serve warm with **crème fraîche**. Serves 6

WEEK 02

BREAKFAST
MARMALADE MUFFINS

Preheat the oven to 180°C/gas mark 4. Line a 12-hole muffin tin with paper cases. In a bowl, mix together **200g self-raising flour, 50g wholemeal flour, 85g golden caster sugar, 1 teaspoon baking powder** and **a pinch of salt**. In a separate large bowl, beat together **1 organic egg, 100g melted butter, 150ml organic milk** and **the zest and juice of 1 lemon**. Gently stir the flour mixture into the egg mixture, followed by **100g marmalade**, taking care not to overmix. If the mixture is too stiff, loosen with another **tablespoon of milk**. Divide the batter equally among the muffin cases and bake in the oven for 25 minutes or until a wooden skewer inserted in the centre comes out clean. Allow to cool slightly and eat warm. Makes 12

PACKED LUNCH
CARIBBEAN RICE AND BEANS

Put **75g long grain rice** in a roomy saucepan with enough **coconut milk** to just cover it. Bring to the boil, season with **salt**, tuck in **a sprig of fresh thyme leaves**, lower the heat, and simmer slowly until all the milk is absorbed. Add water to the rice as it dries to prevent it from sticking. When the rice is perfectly soft, stir in **75g rinsed and drained red kidney beans** and **1 small crushed garlic clove**. Season to taste with **salt** and **freshly ground black pepper**. Serve warm. Serves 1

LUNCH
ROSTI WITH MUSHROOMS

Rösti is a Swiss dish made by forming grated potato into cakes or patties, which are then fried. The outer flakes caramelise delectably during the frying, while the insides remain soft. Mushrooms are an excellent accompaniment to rösti, which soaks up their delicious cooking juices.

5 medium waxy potatoes, peeled
75g butter
3 tablespoons olive oil
2 onions, finely chopped
2 tablespoons freshly chopped parsley
450g closed cup mushrooms, sliced

2 garlic cloves, crushed
2 teaspoons fresh thyme leaves
4 organic eggs
handful of fresh chives, roughly chopped
salt and freshly ground black pepper

SERVES 4

Preheat the oven to 180°C/gas mark 4.

Place the potatoes in a large pan of salted water and bring to the boil. Simmer for 15 minutes, drain and leave until cool enough to handle.

Meanwhile heat 25g butter and 1 tablespoon olive oil in a frying pan, add the onions and cook until soft and starting to turn golden at the edges. Season and tip into a large bowl.

Coarsely grate the potatoes into the bowl with the onions. Add the parsley and season well with salt and freshly ground black pepper. Mix together using your hands and then shape into 8-12 patties and flatten slightly. Heat 25g butter and 1 tablespoon olive oil in a large non-stick frying pan and fry 4 rösti at a time until golden brown on both sides and keep warm in the oven.

Heat the remaining butter and olive oil in a pan and sauté the mushrooms with garlic and thyme on a high heat until tender. Season to taste. Bring a shallow pan of salted water to the boil, reduce the heat and poach the eggs one at a time. Serve each rösti topped with the mushrooms and an egg. Sprinkle with chives, salt and freshly ground black pepper. Serve immediately.

SIDE

POTATO SALAD

Cook **750g small potatoes** in salted boiling water until tender, drain and cool slightly, then cut into bite-size pieces and tip into a large bowl. Trim and finely slice **1 bunch of spring onions**. Cut **6 radishes** into fine matchsticks. Roughly chop **6 cornichons** and **1 tablespoon capers**. In a small bowl whisk together **2 tablespoons wholegrain mustard**, **1 tablespoon white wine vinegar** and **3 tablespoons olive oil** and season with **salt** and **freshly ground black pepper**. Pour the dressing over the potatoes, add the spring onions, radishes, cornichons, capers, **2 tablespoons roughly chopped chives** and **2 tablespoons freshly chopped flatleaf parsley** and gently mix together. Serve at room temperature. Serves 4

DINNER

ROASTED BUTTERNUT SQUASH AND MARROW

ARTHUR POTTS DAWSON

SERVES 4

This recipe combines two totally different kinds of squash. One (the marrow) is delicate and watery. The other (butternut squash) is robust and orange. They look — and taste — very good together.

1 butternut squash, sliced lengthways and seeds scooped out
1 marrow, sliced lengthways and seeds scooped out
2 sprigs of thyme
6 tablespoons olive oil
250g fresh baby spinach leaves
1 romaine lettuce
250g borlotti beans, cooked fresh or canned
100g toasted mixed seeds

FOR THE DRESSING
juice of ½ lemon
1 teaspoon freshly chopped thyme leaves
2 teaspoons honey
2 teaspoons white wine vinegar
salt and freshly ground black pepper

Preheat the oven to 190°C/gas mark 5 . Chop the squash and marrow into thumb-size pieces and arrange in a roasting pan, season with salt and pepper, mix in the thyme sprigs and drizzle with 2–3 tablespoons of the olive oil. Roast in the oven for 25 minutes or until the vegetables are soft to the touch and cooked. Remove from the oven, allow to cool and discard the thyme sprigs.

Wash the spinach and romaine lettuce leaves and dry in a salad spinner. Layer the cooked vegetables, borlotti beans, and mixed seeds in a large salad bowl, placing in the salad leaves as you go. To make the dressing, whisk together the remaining olive oil, lemon juice, thyme leaves, honey and white wine vinegar. Season with salt and freshly ground black pepper and serve drizzled over the salad.

DESSERT

PANNA COTTA

Pour **500ml double cream** into a small saucepan, add the **seeds of 1 vanilla pod**, **zest of 1 lemon** and **40g unrefined golden caster sugar**, then heat gently until the sugar dissolves. Place **2 teaspoons powdered agar-agar** and **2 tablespoons cold water** in a cup or ramekin, stand in a saucepan with a small amount of boiling water in it and allow the agar-agar to dissolve (do not let it get too hot). Take the cream off the heat, remove the lemon zest and whisk the agar-agar into the cream until it dissolves. Pour into 8 individual cups or ramekins. Refrigerate for at least four hours, or overnight, until set. Serves 4

WEEK 03

BREAKFAST

BAKED APPLES WITH YOGURT

Preheat the oven to 180°C/gas mark 4. Core **2 large cooking apples**, fill the centres with **dried cranberries** and **finely grated zest and juice of 1 orange** and drizzle **1 teaspoon runny honey** over the tops. Bake in the oven for 30–40 minutes until tender. Serve with **a couple of dollops of Greek yogurt**. Serves 2

PACKED LUNCH

WILD RICE AND APRICOTS

Preheat the oven to 200°C/gas mark 6. Cook **75g long grain rice** and **75g wild rice** according to the packet instructions. Rinse and refresh in cold water. Roughly chop **125g dried apricots**. Place **50g blanched almonds** on a baking tray and roast in the preheated oven for 2–3 minutes until golden brown. When the nuts are cool, mix together with the rice and apricots, along with **150g natural yogurt**, **75g raisins**, **2 tablespoons finely chopped parsley** and season to taste with salt and freshly ground black pepper. Serves 4–6

LUNCH

CREAMY CELERY SOUP WITH STILTON

SERVES 4

The sharpness of celery combines very well with Stilton, as in this creamy, filling soup. The cheese isn't actually cooked in this recipe – you just crumble it up and pour the hot soup over it.

1 tablespoon olive oil
1 onion, finely chopped
2 large potatoes, peeled and diced
1 head celery, thoroughly washed and roughly chopped
1 teaspoon caraway seeds

1 vegetable stock cube made up with 600ml boiling water
300ml semi-skimmed organic milk
150ml single cream
75g Stilton, crumbled
20g fresh chives, roughly chopped

Heat the oil in a large saucepan then add the onion, potatoes, celery and caraway seeds. Fry gently for approximately 5 minutes until the onion is softened but not coloured.

Add the stock and milk and simmer uncovered for 20–30 minutes. Transfer the soup in batches to a food-processor and whizz until smooth, then return to the rinsed saucepan.

Gently reheat the soup, then stir in the single cream. Do not allow to boil. Crumble the Stilton into individual soup bowls and pour over the soup. Sprinkle with chives and serve immediately with hot, crusty bread.

SNACK

CUCUMBER AND YOGURT DIP

Halve, deseed and grate **1 cucumber** on the coarse side of the grater. Put into a colander and sprinkle with **1–2 teaspoons salt**. Leave to stand for 15 minutes. Drain and dry the cucumber with absorbent kitchen paper. Mix with **300ml Greek yogurt** and **2 teaspoons freshly chopped mint**, and season to taste with **cayenne pepper** and **freshly ground black pepper**. Serve with **crudités**. Serves 6

DINNER

SPLIT PEA DHAL AND CAULIFLOWER CURRY

SERVES 4

An estimated 40 per cent of Indians are vegetarian, so it's no surprise that the nation has perfected the art of meat-free cooking. This recipe proves the point.

FOR THE CURRY

1 rounded teaspoon cumin seeds
1 rounded teaspoon coriander seeds
2 tablespoons sunflower oil
1 onion or 3 shallots, sliced
2 garlic cloves, crushed
1 tablespoon grated fresh ginger
1 green chilli, deseeded and chopped
1 cinnamon stick
½ teaspoon cayenne pepper
½ teaspoon ground turmeric
4 medium size potatoes, peeled and cut
    into chunks
400ml can coconut milk
500ml vegetable stock
227g can tomatoes
½ small cauliflower, cut into florets
handful of green beans, trimmed and cut
    into 4cm lengths

FOR THE DHAL

300g yellow split peas
1 teaspoon ground turmeric
1 cinnamon stick
3 cardamom pods, lightly crushed
2 slices fresh ginger
1 onion, finely chopped
40g butter
1 teaspoon cumin seeds
1 teaspoon coriander seeds
1 red chilli, deseeded and finely chopped
½ tablespoon grated fresh ginger
1 garlic clove, sliced
½ teaspoon kalonji (black onion) seeds
1 teaspoon caster sugar

salt and freshly ground black pepper
coriander leaves to garnish
brown rice to serve

First make the dhal. Tip the split peas into a large bowl, cover with cold water and leave to soak overnight. Drain and rinse the split peas, tip into a saucepan, add the ground turmeric, cinnamon stick, cardamon pods and ginger. Pour over 600ml cold water, bring to the boil, reduce the heat to a very gentle simmer and continue to cook for about 40 minutes until the split peas are very tender and starting to soften at the edges. Season with salt to taste.

Melt the butter in a small frying pan, add the onions and a pinch of salt. Cook over a medium heat until tender but not coloured. Meanwhile lightly crush the cumin and coriander seeds. Add them, along with the chilli, ginger, garlic, kalonji seeds and sugar to the onions and continue to cook until caramelised and fragrant. Serve scattered over the dahl.

To make the curry, heat a small frying pan over a medium heat, add the cumin and coriander seeds and toast for 1 minute or until fragrant. Lightly grind using a pestle and mortar. Heat the oil in a large sauté pan. Add the onion and cook over a medium heat until tender but not coloured. Add the garlic, ginger, chilli and the spices and cook for 1 minute until fragrant.

Add the potatoes to the pan and stir to coat. Pour in the coconut milk, stock and tomatoes and bring to the boil. Reduce the heat and simmer for 5 minutes before adding the cauliflower. Cover and cook over a low heat for 20 minutes until the potato and cauliflower are tender and the sauce has thickened slightly. Add the beans and cook for 2–3 minutes. Season to taste, garnish with coriander and serve with the yellow dahl and brown rice.

DESSERT

LEMON, ALMOND AND PEAR CAKE

Preheat the oven to 180°C/gas mark 4. Line the base of a 20cm springform cake tin with baking parchment. In a bowl cream together **250g softened unsalted butter** and **250g caster sugar**. Beat in **4 large organic egg**s one at a time adding some **plain flour** after each addition (until 50g flour has been added). Fold in **250g ground almonds**, **½ teaspoon almond extract** and the **grated zest** and **juice of 2 lemons**. Spoon the mixture into the tin and smooth the surface. Peel, halve and fan out **4 ripe pears** and place on top of the cake mixture. Bake in the oven for 1 hour or until a skewer inserted into the centre of the cake comes out clean. If the cake seems to be browning too quickly, cover with a piece of foil. Glaze with **4 tablespoons apricot jam** while still warm and allow the cake to cool before removing from the tin. Serves 12

WEEK 04

BREAKFAST

SCRAMBLED EGGS WITH MUSHROOMS

Melt **15g butter** in a small saucepan over a low heat. Add **50g button or chestnut mushrooms**, cover with a lid and cook gently until soft. Meanwhile, beat **2 organic eggs** in a bowl and season with **salt** and **freshly ground black pepper**. Melt a further **25g butter** in a non-stick frying pan set over a medium heat until foaming. Pour in the beaten eggs and let them sit for 10 seconds. Scramble using a wooden spoon until the eggs are cooked but still soft, taking care not to overstir. Spoon onto a plate with the mushrooms and serve immediately. Serves 1

PACKED LUNCH

LENTILS WITH TAHINI DIP

Soak **100g brown lentils** overnight, drain and rinse thoroughly. Place them in a saucepan with **1 lightly crushed garlic clove** and **1 small peeled onion**. Cover with water and bring to the boil, cooking for 10 minutes; then cover the pan and continue to cook for a further 40 minutes until the lentils are tender. Crush **1 garlic clove** and mix it with **2 tablespoons tahini paste** and **1 tablespoon lemon juice**, some **salt** and **freshly ground black pepper** to make a thick cream. Add a few drops of **cold water** if it is too stiff. Put the lentils, onion and garlic in a blender and add **1 tablespoon lemon juice** and **1 tablespoon freshly chopped flatleaf parsley**. Whizz to purée. Taste and adjust the seasoning if necessary and turn out into a serving dish. Dust with **paprika** and sprinkle over **1 tablespoon finely chopped flatleaf parsley**. Make a small well in the middle and add a little more tahini paste. Serve with **hot pitta** and **black olives**. Serves 2

LUNCH

FENNEL SAUTEED WITH PEPPERS

SERVES 2

Fennel is one of the stronger-tasting vegetables. Some people find its aniseedy flavour a bit overpowering when it is raw but frying it with sweet red peppers, garlic and peas takes the edge off it. It comes in fat, dense bulbs.

2 tablespoons olive oil
2 red peppers, deseeded and cut into
    thin strips
500g fennel, trimmed and finely chopped,
    (about 3 bulbs)
2 garlic cloves, crushed
250g peas, shelled
salt and freshly ground black pepper
1 tablespoon freshly chopped flatleaf parsley

In a wok or heavy-bottomed frying pan heat the oil, add the peppers and fennel and cook for 10–15 minutes over a moderate heat until crunchy, stirring occasionally. Add the garlic and peas and continue cooking for 2 minutes. Season, scatter with the parsley and serve.

SNACK
BABA GHANOUSH

Preheat the oven to 200°C/gas mark 6. Prick **2 medium size aubergines** with a fork several times and place on a lightly greased baking tray. Bake for 35-40 minutes, until the skins are wrinkled and the flesh is soft. Soak **1 slice brown bread** in **a little water** and squeeze out. Set aside. Cut the aubergines in half lengthways and use a spoon to scoop out the flesh from the skin. In a food-processor, purée the aubergines with **3 crushed garlic cloves**, the soaked bread, **juice of ½ lemon**, **2 teaspoons cumin** and **5 tablespoons olive oil** until smooth and creamy. Stir in **3 tablespoons Greek yogurt** and pile into a large bowl. Scatter with **a handful of freshly chopped flatleaf parsley** and **2 tablespoons stoned and quartered black olives**. Serve with **vegetable crudités** and **toasted pitta**. Serves 4

DINNER
WALNUT AND MUSHROOM RISOTTO

SERVES 4

This is a very autumnal risotto, perfect on a windy evening when the nights are drawing in. It's better to buy your nutmegs whole rather than powdered — they lose their flavour much more slowly and the gratings always taste fresh.

400g uncooked long grain rice
2 tablespoons olive oil or 25g butter
1 onion, finely chopped
250g large flat mushrooms, chopped
75g walnuts, roughly chopped
6 cloves

¼ teaspoon grated nutmeg
100ml white wine
1 tablespoon double cream
freshly chopped parsley, to garnish
salt and freshly ground black pepper

Cook the rice in a large pan of boiling salted water according to the packet instructions.

Heat the olive oil or butter in a large saucepan, add the onion and fry gently for 5-10 minutes until it begins to brown. Add the mushrooms, walnuts and spices and cook for 5 minutes, or until the mushrooms have begun to soften, adding a little more oil or butter if necessary. Add the wine, season with salt and freshly ground black pepper and simmer for a further 2 minutes until the mushrooms are tender. Stir in the rice and cream and heat through gently, stirring constantly. Remove the cloves and serve hot, garnished with freshly chopped parsley.

DESSERT
APPLE CAKE

Preheat the oven to 180°C/gas mark 4. Line a 20cm, springform tin with baking parchment. Whizz **125g butter and 175g caster sugar** in a mixer until creamy, soft and pale in colour. Add **3 organic eggs**, one at a time, beating gently after each addition. Stir **1 teaspoon baking powder** into **175g plain flour** and add this to the egg mixture. At this stage, add **1 tablespoon organic milk** if desired and stir in **a few drops of vanilla extract**. Peel and core **2 medium Bramley apples** and cut them into slices, around 3-4cm thick. Put a layer of cake mixture at the base of the tin. Arrange a layer of apples on top, then sprinkle with **1 tablespoon of sultanas**. Repeat, and finish with a layer of the cake mixture. Bake in the centre of the oven for 35-40 minutes, until cooked through. Turn out onto a wire tray, peel the baking parchment and allow to cool. Dust with **icing sugar**. Serve at room temperature. Serves 6-8

WEEK 05

BREAKFAST

FRUITY QUINOA

A delicious alternative to porridge. In a small saucepan bring **250ml almond milk** and **½ teaspoon vanilla extract** to the boil. Stir in **50g quinoa**, reduce the heat to low and simmer gently for 10 minutes or until most of the liquid has been absorbed. Remove from the heat and stir in **50g blackberries** and **1 tablespoon chopped pecans**. Spoon into 2 bowls and drizzle with **runny honey**. Serves 2

PACKED LUNCH

BASIL AND MUSHROOM TART

SERVES 4–6

Cèpes are low in fat and high in protein, vitamins, minerals and dietary fibre making a healthy and tasty filling for a tart. Pâte brisée is the French equivalent of shortcrust pastry.

FOR THE PATE BRISEE
120g plain flour
60g butter, cubed
1 organic egg yolk
1–2 tablespoons cold water
a pinch of salt

FOR THE MUSHROOM FILLING
180g cèpes, or other small cap wild
*   mushrooms or button mushrooms*
50g unsalted butter
2 small shallots, finely chopped
1 tablespoon plain flour
150ml single cream
salt and freshly ground black pepper
1 tablespoon freshly chopped basil leaves
2 sprigs parsley

Preheat the oven to 200°C/gas mark 6.

Start by making the pastry. Run the flour through a sieve into a bowl and make a well in the centre. Add the butter, egg yolk and water, along with the pinch of salt and work in the flour and the rest of the ingredients. Form into a ball, using a little extra flour if necessary. Wrap the pastry in clingfilm and replace in the bowl, chilling in the fridge for 30 minutes.

In the meantime, clean the mushrooms carefully of any dirt and dry them with a cloth; quarter any larger ones. In a heavy-bottomed pan melt the butter and toss in the mushrooms and shallots, stirring for 3–4 minutes until they are soft. Remove with a slotted spoon and keep warm, reserving the juices.

Roll out the pastry on a lightly-floured, cold surface and line a 24cm tart tin. Prick the base of the pastry, line with baking parchment and baking beans and bake in the oven for 8–10 minutes.

As the pastry case is cooking, put the juices from the mushroom pan back onto the heat, stir in the flour and, over a moderate heat, cook gently for 2 minutes. Then add the cream and allow to thicken, stirring all the time. Season with salt and pepper and add the basil.

Assemble the tart by discarding the baking parchment and baking beans. Then arrange the mushrooms on the base of the tart, pour over the sauce and put the tart tin back into the oven to heat through, allowing around 10 minutes. Once the filling is lightly set, remove and decorate with the parsley leaves and serve. Delicious with a plain green salad.

LUNCH
EASY EGG FLORENTINE

Preheat the oven to 180°C/gas mark 4. Lightly grease a large ramekin dish or teacup with **butter**. Defrost **50g frozen spinach**, squeeze out all excess water, season with **salt** and **freshly ground black pepper**, and spoon into the base of the ramekin dish, making a slight well in the centre. Break **2 organic eggs** into the dish, dot with more **butter**, pour over **1 tablespoon cream** and sprinkle with **1 tablespoon freshly grated vegetarian Parmesan**. Bake in the oven for 10 minutes until the edges of the egg whites are just beginning to set and the yolks are firm. Serves 1

SIDE
SHALLOTS GLAZED WITH ORANGE

Take **12 medium size shallots** and trim them but do not peel. Arrange them in a single layer in a shallow baking tray and drizzle over some **extra virgin olive oil**, along with **2-3 sprigs lemon thyme**. Roast in a preheated oven, 200°C/gas mark 6, for 45 minutes or so. They are cooked when the shallots are tender; remove from the oven and, with a couple of forks, ease the shallots from their skins. Discard the thyme. Put the shallots back in the pan with **the juice and zest of 1 orange**, together with **1-2 teaspoons brown sugar** and put back in the oven and allow to dissolve and brown. This should take 5-10 minutes. Serves 3-4

DINNER
PENNE WITH BROCCOLI, MASCARPONE AND DOLCELATTE

SERVES 4

It isn't immediately obvious why the Italians call short tubes of pasta cut at an angle penne (feathers) but if you look at the nib of an old fashioned quill the name starts to make sense. Brassicas and cheeses often go well together. Here, broccoli is combined with sweet, creamy mascarpone and dolcelatte to make an irresistible sauce, which oozes into the penne and sticks to their ridged sides.

500g broccoli, chopped into small florets
50g mascarpone
200g dolcelatte
2 tablespoons crème fraîche
1 tablespoon balsamic vinegar
1 tablespoon dry white wine
400g penne
2 tablespoons capers
4 tablespoons black olives
1 tablespoon hazelnuts, crushed and toasted
salt and freshly ground black pepper

Steam the broccoli florets over a pan of boiling water for 4–5 minutes. Run under cold water and set aside.

In a heavy pan, gently heat the mascarpone, dolcelatte, crème fraîche, vinegar and wine. Add the broccoli florets.

Cook the pasta in boiling salted water until it is just tender, drain well, return to the pan and pour over the hot sauce. Sprinkle with capers, olives, and hazelnuts and toss well. Adjust the seasoning and serve.

DESSERT
PLUM CRUMBLE

Preheat the oven to 190°C /gas mark 5. Halve and stone **500g plums** and place in an ovenproof dish along with **1 tablespoon water**. Put **125g plain wholemeal flour** in a mixing bowl, add **75g butter** and rub it in with your fingertips until the mixture resembles fine breadcrumbs. Stir in **50g caster sugar**, sprinkle the crumble mixture over the top of the fruit and bake in the oven for 25–30 minutes. Serve hot with **yogurt** or **fromage frais**. Serves 4

WEEK 06

BREAKFAST

SPICED PUMPKIN CREPES

Sift **100g plain flour** into a bowl. Add **1 teaspoon baking powder**, **25g caster sugar** and **1/2 teaspoon ground allspice**, **1/2 teaspoon cinnamon** and stir to combine. In a separate, large, bowl, whisk together **60ml organic milk**, **150g canned pumpkin or pumpkin purée**, **1 organic egg yolk**, **25g melted butter** and **1 teaspoon vanilla extract**. Add the dry ingredients, and beat until until you have a smooth, thick batter. In another bowl, whisk **1 organic egg white** until soft peaks form. Fold into the pumpkin mixture. Pour **a little oil** into a non-stick frying pan set over a medium heat. Working in batches, ladle 3–4 spoonfuls of the mixture into the frying pan and cook until bubbles form on the surface of the crêpes, and the bottoms are golden, about 1–2 minutes each side. Serves 6

PACKED LUNCH

VEGGIE SAUSAGE SANDWICH

Drizzle **2 slices of sourdough bread** with a little **olive oil** and toast lightly on both sides. Heat a little olive oil in a pan and add **1/2 chopped red onion**. Allow the onion to sweat. When it starts to wilt, add **1/4 teaspoon sugar**, **a pinch of salt**, some **freshly ground black pepper** and **1 teaspoon balsamic vinegar**. Cook for a further 3–4 minutes. Now, start to cook **2 vegetarian sausages** in a frying pan with a little olive oil. When they are coloured on all sides, turn down the heat and cook for a further 6–8 minutes. Halve **2 baby plum tomatoes** and place in the pan with the onions. Add a little water and **1/4 teaspoon of sugar** and **1 teaspoon balsamic vinegar**, season again, and allow to reduce a little on a medium heat. To assemble, cut the cooked sausages in half lengthways. Spoon the tomato and onion mix over 1 slice of the bread and place the sausages on top. Top with the remaining slice of bread. Serves 1

LUNCH

CREAMY MUSHROOM SOUP

SERVES 4

Field mushrooms are grown year round in climate-controlled conditions but early autumn is their natural season. This simple recipe brings out their delicate, earthy qualities to the full.

75g butter
4 shallots, finely chopped
1 garlic clove, crushed
500g field mushrooms, cleaned and sliced
1 litre vegetable stock
1 tablespoon plain flour

TO SERVE
soy sauce
thick cream
salt and freshly ground black pepper

Heat 50g of the butter in a heavy-bottomed pan and sauté the shallots until softened; add the garlic and cook for 1 minute more. Add the mushrooms and stir to coat well. Pour in the stock and bring to the boil. Season and cover, simmering for 10–15 minutes, until the mushrooms are cooked. Remove from the heat.

In a separate pan, heat the remaining butter and stir in the flour to make a roux. Cook for 2 minutes and remove from the stove. In a liquidiser, blend the roux with the soup (this may need to be done in batches). Return the soup to the pan, bring back to the boil, add the soy sauce to taste, check the seasoning and stir in a dollop or 2 of cream.

SNACK

CRANBERRY AND APRICOT FLAPJACKS

Preheat the oven to 180°C/gas mark 4. Grease a 20cm square baking tin. In a saucepan over a low heat, gently heat **125g butter, 100g soft brown sugar** and **2 tablespoons golden syrup** until the sugar has dissolved. Stir in **200g rolled oats, a pinch of salt, 25g dried cranberries, 25g dried chopped apricots** and mix well. Spoon into the prepared tin and smooth level. Bake for 30 minutes until golden. Remove from the oven, cut into squares and leave to cool completely before removing from the tin. Makes 16 squares

DINNER

SAUTEED AUBERGINES AND MOZZARELLA

SERVES 4

Aubergines were cultivated by the Chinese as long ago as the 5th century BC and the Moors introduced them into Europe. Try the many varieties and colours of aubergines now available.

4 small, long, thin aubergines
1 garlic clove, crushed
1 tablespoon freshly chopped parsley
50g toasted breadcrumbs
3 tablespoons olive oil
150g buffalo mozzarella, cut into 5mm slices
1 tablespoon Greek basil leaves
salt and freshly ground black pepper

Preheat the oven to 190°C /gas mark 6.

Cut the aubergines in half length. Score the flesh deeply, but do not cut the skin. Arrange in a shallow pan, skin-side down.

Mix together the garlic, parsley, breadcrumbs and half the olive oil, season, and press the mixture into the scored aubergines.

Drizzle over the rest of the oil and place in the oven until golden. Remove from the oven, arrange the mozzarella on top, and return to the oven for a further 5 minutes or until the cheese has melted. Scatter with Greek basil to serve.

DESSERT

GINGERBREAD CAKE

Preheat the oven to 170°C /gas mark 3 and lightly grease and flour a 15cm cake tin. Cream **115g butter** and **115g sugar** together in a large mixing bowl. Add **1 organic egg** a little at a time, beating between each addition. Mix together **225g self-raising flour, 1/2 teaspoon ground cinnamon, 2 teaspoons ground ginger, 1/4 teaspoon nutmeg** and add them to the butter mixture. Gradually add **120ml organic milk**, stirring to make a smooth batter. Warm **2 tablespoons black treacle** slightly and then beat it into the batter. Transfer the batter to the cake tin and bake for 40–45 minutes. Serves 6

WEEK 07

BREAKFAST

AVOCADO ON TOAST

Toast **2 slices of wholemeal bread** and spread with **butter**. Mash **1/2 avocado** onto the toast with a fork and season with **salt** and **freshly ground black pepper**. Drizzle **a little extra virgin olive oil** over the top if you wish. Serves 1

PACKED LUNCH

TUSCAN BEAN AND VEGETABLE SOUP

This hearty soup is perfect for a windy autumn day and takes less than half an hour to make. Make sure you serve it with good, crusty bread.

25g butter
1 tablespoon olive oil
1 medium onion, finely chopped
1 garlic clove, peeled and finely chopped
1 stick celery, trimmed and finely chopped
1 large carrot, peeled and finely chopped
425g can mixed bean salad, drained
400g can chopped tomatoes

900ml vegetable stock
1 teaspoon dried oregano
2 tablespoons pesto sauce, plus extra
*   to garnish*
2 medium courgettes, trimmed and finely
*   chopped*
2 tablespoons soured cream
salt and freshly ground black pepper

SERVES 4

Melt the butter with the oil in a large saucepan and gently fry the chopped onion, garlic, celery and carrot for 5 minutes until just tender.

Stir in the beans, tomatoes and stock. Add the oregano, pesto and season to taste. Bring to the boil and simmer for 10 minutes. Add the courgettes to the soup. Cook for a further 5 minutes until all the vegetables are tender. Ladle the soup into warmed bowls and top with the soured cream and pesto sauce.

LUNCH

RED AND YELLOW PEPPER SALAD

Place **75g couscous** in a wide shallow bowl and cover with **100ml boiling water**. Fork through, then cover tightly with a tea towel. Leave to stand for about 20 minutes. Meanwhile, preheat the grill. Chop **1/2 red and 1/2 yellow pepper** into large chunks and remove the seeds and membrane. Place on a sheet of foil on a grill tray and grill for about 5-10 minutes until charred and blistered. Remove from the grill and wrap tightly in the foil. Leave for about 15 minutes to loosen the skin. Then remove the skin and wipe with kitchen paper, and cut into dice. Fork through the couscous to remove any lumps. Whisk together **1 1/2 tablespoons olive oil, 1 teaspoon white wine vinegar, 1 crushed garlic clove, salt** and **freshly ground black pepper** and pour over the couscous. Stir well, then allow to cool. Once cool, add the peppers and some **freshly chopped basil leaves** and stir. Check the seasoning and serve at room temperature. Serves 2

SIDE

STIR-FRIED CABBAGE

Cut **1 onion** into thin slices and fry in **1 tablespoon olive oil** until crisp. Set aside. Heat **25g butter** and **1 tablespoon olive oil** in a large frying pan or wok, add **150g chopped cabbage** and stir-fry for 2–3 minutes. Sprinkle over the crispy onion and serve. Serves 2

DINNER

TOMATO, FETA, ALMOND AND DATE BAKLAVA

MARIA ELIA

SERVES 4

The distinction between main courses and desserts is vaguer in the Near East than in Western Europe. Baklava is a flaky filo pastry dish popular from Greece to Central Asia. It's most familiar in its sweet form, filed with chopped pistachio nuts and drenched in honey or syrup, but this savoury version is just as good.

7 tablespoons olive oil
5 Spanish onions, halved and finely chopped
2 garlic cloves, finely chopped
2 teaspoons ground cinnamon
a pinch of sugar
a bunch of dill, finely chopped
 (or 3 teaspoons dried)
8 plum tomatoes, peeled and roughly
 chopped (reserve half of the juices)

3 teaspoons tomato purée
9 large sheets filo pastry
150ml melted butter
7 tablespoons blanched almonds,
 whizzed to a crumble
4 Medjool dates, stoned and finely sliced
 (any variety of dates can be used)
250g feta
6 tablespoons honey

Preheat the oven to 180°C/gas mark 4. Heat the olive oil in a large, wide pan. Gently fry the onions over low heat, add the garlic, cinnamon and sugar and increase the heat. Fry for about 6 minutes, until caramelised. Add the dill, tomatoes and juices, plus the tomato purée and cook for about 5 minutes longer, until reduced.

Unfold the filo sheets and cut them in half; keep them covered with a damp cloth to prevent them from drying out. Brush a baking tray (about 20 x 30cm) with melted butter, line the pan with a sheet of filo, brush with butter and repeat until you have a 3-layer thickness.

Spread half the onion mixture over the pastry, top with half the almonds, the dates and half the feta. Sandwich 3 layers of filo together, brushing each with melted butter and place on top of the onion and feta mix. Top with the remaining onions, almonds and feta and again top with a 3-layer thickness of filo, lightly score the top, cutting diamonds or squares, brush with butter and splash with a little water. Bake for 30–35 minutes until golden. Let cool a little before serving, then drizzle each portion with honey.

DESSERT

PEARS POACHED WITH STAR ANISE

Peel and core **8 firm dessert pears** and cut them in half. Put them into a bowl and sprinkle over the **juice of 1/2 lemon**, tossing well. Heat **400ml water** in a large pan and stir in **75g granulated sugar** until it dissolves completely. Add **5 star anise** and just simmer for 5 minutes to infuse. Then add the pears and bring to the boil. Simmer, covered, until the pears are al dente, stirring a couple of times. Remove the pears with a slotted spoon and keep warm. Keep the pan on the stove and turn up the heat to high, boiling to reduce the poaching liquor by about half. Pour in **2 tablespoons Pernod** and leave to cook for a couple of minutes. Run the liquor through a sieve onto the pears and serve. Serves 4–6

WEEK 08

BREAKFAST

BIRCHER MUESLI WITH APPLE

A healthy breakfast that will keep hunger pangs at bay until lunchtime. In a bowl, mix together **100g rolled oats, 1 tablespoon pumpkin seeds, 1 tablespoon sunflower seeds** and **25g dried apricots**. Pour over **150ml apple juice** and ideally chill for at least an hour or overnight. When ready to serve, core **1 eating apple** and coarsely grate it into the bowl (there's no need to peel it) and stir it into the oat mixture, together with **1 tablespoon toasted almonds**. Spoon the mixture into two serving bowls, loosening it with a little more apple juice if it is too thick. Top each with **1 tablespoon of Greek yogurt** and drizzle with **runny honey**. Serves 2

PACKED LUNCH

PEAR, WALNUT AND STILTON SALAD

Peel and core **1 ripe pear**, slice lengthways into thin segments, toss in the **juice of 1/2 lemon** and place in a bowl. Add **15g rocket, 1 tablespoon chopped toasted walnuts, 25g Stilton** and some **freshly ground black pepper**. Whisk together **3 teaspoons walnut oil, 1 teaspoon white wine vinegar** and **a pinch of salt** and drizzle over the salad. Serves 1

LUNCH

PASTA WITH BROCCOLI, SUN-DRIED TOMATOES AND OLIVES

LIVIA FIRTH

SERVES 4

Orecchiette means 'little ears' and that's exactly what the pasta scoops used in this recipe resemble. This dish only has 6 ingredients and takes minutes to make but the broccoli ensures that it is very tasty.

olive oil
2 garlic cloves, finely chopped
1 tablespoon sun-dried tomatoes
3 heads of broccoli, chopped into small florets
1 tablespoon black olives, stoned
1 tablespoon pine nuts
500g orecchiette pasta
salt
freshly grated vegetarian Parmesan, to serve

Heat the olive oil in a saucepan and add the garlic. Let the garlic brown on a slow heat, then turn off and add the sun-dried tomatoes.

Fill a large saucepan with water and bring to the boil, add salt, then the broccoli and let it boil very tender. Remove the broccoli from the pan with a slotted spoon and add to the saucepan with the garlic, sun-dried tomatoes, olives and pine nuts. Put the pan over a low heat and crush the broccoli with a fork until it is mashed.

Add the pasta to the water where the broccoli has been boiled. Cook the pasta until al dente then drain and stir it in with the broccoli sauce and serve with some grated Parmesan scattered over the top.

SNACK

SWEET AND SOUR TOFU

Preheat the oven to 200°C/gas mark 6. Mix **75ml light soy sauce**, **25g chopped lemongrass**, **1 thinly sliced red chilli**, **30ml white wine vinegar**, **25ml sesame oil** and **2 teaspoons runny honey** in a bowl to make a sweet and sour sauce. Put **1 carrot**, **1 stick of celery**, **1cm piece of peeled ginger** and **1 garlic clove** into a food-processor and whizz at high speed, pulsing until the vegetables are finely chopped but not puréed. Make deep slashes in the narrow sides of **2 x 100g fried tofu slices** to create a pocket, and stuff with the vegetable mixture. Arrange the slices in a baking dish, pour over the sweet and sour sauce and bake for 15–20 minutes. Serves 2

DINNER

THAI VEGETABLE CURRY

In just a few decades, Thai food has grown from relative obscurity into one of the most popular cuisines on Earth. This vegetable curry has many of its classic tastes and textures.

FOR THE CURRY PASTE
2 shallots, roughly chopped
2 garlic cloves, finely chopped
1 tablespoon freshly grated ginger
1 stick lemongrass, finely chopped
2 green chillies, deseeded and chopped
zest of 1 lime
small bunch fresh coriander

1 tablespoon sunflower oil
1 small aubergine, cut into chunks
1 red pepper, deseeded and cut into dice
8 chestnut mushrooms, halved (or quartered if large)

400ml can coconut milk
6 okra, cut on the diagonal into 3 pieces
8 baby corn, cut on the diagonal into 3 pieces
150g canned bamboo shoots, drained
handful of sugar snaps, cut in half on the diagonal
2 handfuls of beansprouts
soy sauce
palm or soft light brown sugar to taste

TO SERVE
fresh coriander leaves
jasmine rice
lime wedges

SERVES 4

Prepare the curry paste first. Place the shallots, garlic and ginger in a food-processor. Add the lemongrass, chillies, lime zest and coriander stalks (reserving the leaves) and whizz the mixture until finely chopped. You can also make this paste using a pestle and mortar if you prefer.

Heat the sunflower oil in a large sauté pan. Add the curry paste and cook over a medium heat for 1 minute until the mixture smells fragrant. Add the aubergine, red pepper and mushrooms and cook for 1 minute stirring frequently until starting to become tender. Add the coconut milk to the pan with 150ml of water and bring to the boil. Add the okra, baby corn and bamboo shoots and continue to cook for a further 5 minutes or so until the veggies are tender. Finally add the sugar snaps and beansprouts to the pan and cook for another 30 seconds.

Taste and add a dash of soy sauce or teaspoon of sugar if needed. Serve the curry in bowls, garnished with coriander leaves and with jasmine rice and lime wedges to squeeze over.

DESSERT

FLORENTINES

Preheat the oven to 180°C/gas mark 4. Line a baking tray with baking parchment. Mix together **50g chopped flaked almonds**, **25g chopped hazelnuts**, **25g chopped mixed peel**, **50g chopped glacé cherries** and **50g seedless raisins**. Melt **75g butter** in a saucepan, stir in **75g soft light brown sugar** and heat gently, stirring until the sugar has dissolved. Continue to heat until the mixture just starts to bubble. Remove from the heat and stir in the fruit and nuts. Place spoonfuls of the mixture onto the baking tray, leaving sufficient space between each for spreading. Bake in batches for 10–12 minutes until golden. As soon as the tray is removed from the oven, use a knife to tidy any uneven edges. Allow to cool a little. When firm, place on a cooling rack until cold. Melt **75g plain chocolate** and **75g white chocolate** and use to coat the flat side of the Florentines, using plain chocolate on half the Florentines and white chocolate on the others. Using a fork, draw wavy lines on the chocolate. Leave until set. Makes 16

WEEK 09

BREAKFAST

BREAKFAST FRITTATA

Peel and slice **1 large potato**, place in a pan of water, bring to the boil then drain thoroughly. Pat the potato dry with kitchen paper. Crack **4 organic eggs** into a bowl, season with **salt** and **freshly ground black pepper**, and whisk lightly. Place a small frying pan over a medium heat, pour in **2 tablespoons olive oil** and add **1 finely chopped onion** and the sliced potato. Cook for 10 minutes until golden, then add to the bowl of eggs. Put the frying pan back on a low heat, add another **tablespoon of olive oil**, and pour in the egg mixture. Cook for about 10 minutes or until the egg mixture has set. If you like, arrange some **tomato slices** on top, then place under a preheated grill for 5 minutes until it is golden. Serves 2

PACKED LUNCH

ROAST VEGETABLE TART

Slice **1 large red onion** into chunky pieces. Slice **3 yellow peppers** into thick strips. Cut **1 aubergine** lengthways into 2cm thick slices. Peel **4 garlic cloves**. Combine in a roasting tin and drizzle with **olive oil**. Season with **salt** and **freshly ground black pepper** and scatter over some **fresh thyme leaves**. Roast in oven preheated to 200°C/gas mark 6 for 30 minutes until the vegetables are soft. Remove the garlic, slice thinly and return to the tin. Roll out **375g puff pastry** into a rectangle roughly 30 x 15cm and place on a baking sheet. Spread with **3 tablespoons sundried tomato paste**, top with the roast vegetables and **1 tablespoon chopped black olives**. Crumble over **200g goat's cheese**. Bake in the oven for 20 minutes until the pastry is crisp and the cheese is golden brown. Serve with a green salad. Serves 4

LUNCH

LEEK AND GOAT'S CHEESE QUICHE

BRYN WILLIAMS

SERVES 4

The sweetness of leeks combines very well with the tartness of goat's cheese in this nicely uncomplicated quiche. The real genius of this recipe, though, is the curry power. It isn't the most obvious ingredient for a dish originating in France but it works a touch of magic.

200g shortcrust pastry
20g butter
1 teaspoon curry powder
2 leeks, trimmed and finely sliced

6 organic eggs
700ml double cream
100g goat's cheese
salt and freshly ground black pepper

Preheat the oven to 160°C/gas mark 3.

Roll out the shortcrust pastry into a 25cm quiche tin, leave to rest for 1 hour, and then bake blind for 25 minutes.

Add the butter to a saucepan, then add the leeks, season with salt and freshly ground black pepper and add the curry powder. Cook the leeks until soft but not coloured.

Break the eggs into a large bowl and gently whisk in the double cream. Crumble in the goat's cheese and season with salt and freshly ground black pepper.

Place the cooked leeks into the quiche tin. Pour in the egg mixture and bake for 35–45 minutes or until cooked.

SIDE
LEMON BROCCOLI

Heat a little **olive oil** in a large pan and cook **1 sliced garlic clove** until softened. Add **200g blanched broccoli** and **the zest and juice of ½ lemon** and heat through. Season to taste with **salt** and **freshly ground black pepper**. Serves 2–3

DINNER
CHICKPEA TAGINE WITH HARISSA

SERVES 4

Strictly speaking, a tagine should be cooked in a traditional North African earthenware pot of the same name. One of the beauties of this recipe is that you don't actually need one to make it. Another is that it is extremely Moorish, if you'll pardon the pun. Harissa is a spicy paste made from chilli, garlic and various other seasonings. You can buy it ready-made in the shops.

1 large onion, finely chopped
2 carrots, peeled
1 large sweet potato, peeled and
    cut into chunks
1 red pepper, deseeded and diced
1 stick celery, chopped
1 courgette, chopped
1 teaspoon cumin seeds
1 teaspoon coriander seeds
a pinch of saffron strands
2 tablespoons olive oil
2 garlic cloves, crushed

1 tablespoon grated fresh ginger
1 cinnamon stick
227g can chopped tomatoes
700ml vegetable stock
400g can chickpeas, drained
1 tablespoon clear honey
salt and freshly ground black pepper

TO SERVE
wholewheat or barley couscous
harissa

Prepare the vegetables.

Tip the cumin and coriander seeds into a small dry frying pan and toast over a medium heat for 30 seconds until fragrant. Lightly grind using a pestle and mortar. Soak the saffron strands in 1 tablespoon of boiling water.

Heat the olive oil in a large sauté pan over a medium heat. Add the onion and cook for 3–4 minutes until tender but not coloured. Add the ground spices, garlic, grated ginger and cinnamon stick and continue to cook for a further minute. Add the chopped tomatoes and tip the vegetables and the drained chickpeas into the pan. Stir to coat the veggies in the spiced mixture and pour over the stock. Bring to the boil, reduce the heat to a gentle simmer and continue to cook for 20–25 minutes until the vegetables are tender. Add the honey and season with salt and freshly ground black pepper.

Serve in bowls with couscous and a good spoonful of harissa.

DESSERT
APPLE SYLLABUB

Peel, core and chop **3 Golden Delicious apples** and place in a saucepan. Add **2 tablespoons water** and **1 tablespoon caster sugar** to the saucepan, cover and cook for 8–10 minutes or until soft. Allow to cool. Place **150ml sweet white wine**, **zest** and **juice of 1 lemon**, **50g caster sugar** and **300ml double cream** in a bowl and whisk until the mixture holds its shape. Carefully fold in the apple purée and spoon into 6 tall glasses. Allow to chill for 1–2 hours, then decorate with **fresh mint sprigs** and **apple slices**. Serves 6

WEEK 10

BREAKFAST

POACHED QUINCE WITH VANILLA

Dissolve **250g granulated sugar** in **500ml water** slowly and then, when the sugar is melted, bring to the boil and make a syrup, cooking for 2 minutes. Meantime, peel, core and quarter **4 ripe quinces**, and slip them into the hot syrup, together with **6 cloves**. Simmer for about 35–40 minutes and serve, together with some **natural yogurt**, if you like. Serves 4

PACKED LUNCH

PUY LENTILS AND ROASTED RED PEPPERS WITH GOAT'S CHEESE

SERVES 4

People have been cooking with lentils for ten thousand years. Rich in protein and vitamins, they perform a vital dietary role in some of the poorest parts of the world. Many cooks consider Puy lentils to be the best variety. They are a beautiful greeny blue and have a unique, peppery flavour.

3 red peppers
175g Puy lentils
1 red onion, whole
sprig each of fresh parsley, oregano and thyme
4 tablespoons sun-dried tomatoes, chopped
100g crumbled goat's cheese

4 tablespoons freshly chopped parsley, oregano and thyme
4 tablespoons extra virgin olive oil
1 tablespoons lemon juice
salt and freshly ground black pepper

Roast the peppers on a baking tray in an oven preheated to 200°C/gas mark 6, for 30 minutes. Put them into a polythene bag. When cooled, deseed and peel the peppers, then cut them into strips. Set aside.

Wash the Puy lentils thoroughly and cook them, covered in 350ml water, with the whole onion and herbs. These lentils cook faster than other types, in about 15 minutes. Drain. Roughly chop the onion and add back into the lentils. Discard the herbs. While still warm, add the tomatoes and goat's cheese and stir gently. Season.

Make the dressing, by combining the rest of the ingredients. Pour over the lentil mixture and mix well. Arrange the lentils with the slices of red pepper on individual plates. Sprinkle with the herbs and serve.

LUNCH

CHEESE AND CHIVE POTATO JACKETS

Preheat the oven to 200°C/gas mark 6. Place **4 medium baking potatoes** on a baking tray and cook for 1 1/2 hours until soft. Remove from the oven, cut in half and scoop out the potato into a bowl. Combine with **25g butter** and **100ml warmed organic milk** to achieve a smooth creamy mash. Stir in **100g grated Cheddar** and **2 tablespoons chives**. Whisk **4 organic egg whites** in a bowl until they form soft peaks. Fold the egg whites into the mashed potato and spoon back into the potato skins. Return to the oven and cook for 10–15 minutes or until golden brown and well risen. A good green salad goes excellently. Serves 4

SIDE
HERB BREAD

Preheat an oven to 180°C/gas mark 4. Slice a stone-baked **baguette** along its length, taking care not to cut all the way through. Melt **75g butter**, stir in **2 tablespoons freshly chopped parsley**, **1 tablespoon freshly chopped basil or oregano** and **1 crushed garlic clove**, then spread along the inside of each cut in the bread. Wrap in foil and bake for 10 minutes. Serves 4

DINNER
TAGLIATELLE WITH MUSHROOM SAUCE

SERVES 4

Porcini ('little pigs' in Italian) are known as cèpes in France and Penny Buns in some parts of England. They are dense, almost meaty wild mushrooms with pores on their undersides instead of gills. Drying them concentrates the forest-like taste. They give this lovely pasta dish its considerable depth of flavour.

40g dried porcini mushrooms
2 tablespoons olive oil
1 large onion, finely chopped
250g chestnut mushrooms, cut into quarters
450g tagliatelle

150g dolcelatte, crumbled
handful of flatleaf parsley, finely snipped
salt and freshly ground black pepper

Put the porcini into a bowl and pour over 500ml of boiling water. Leave them to soak and soften for about half an hour. Then drain and gently squeeze out any excess water from the porcini.

In a frying pan, heat the oil and add the onion, cooking for 5 minutes until translucent and soft but not coloured. Add the chestnut mushrooms and coat them well in the olive oil, then cover the pan and leave to release their juices, shaking occasionally, for about 15–20 minutes. Chop the porcini finely and stir them into the pan. Continue cooking for about 10 minutes and season with a little salt and freshly ground black pepper.

Meantime set a large pot of salted, cold water to boil and cook the pasta until al dente. Drain well and put into a large serving bowl. Check the seasoning of the mushroom sauce and pour it over the tagliatelle, followed by the dolcelatte. Stir gently to mix the sauce — the heat will melt the dolcelatte. Sprinkle over the parsley and serve.

DESSERT
CARROT CAKE

STELLA McCARTNEY

Grease the insides of two 20cm cake tins and line the bases with a disc of buttered baking parchment. Preheat the oven to 180°C/gas mark 4. Tip **100g walnuts** into a small roasting tin and toast in the preheated oven for 5 minutes. Reserve a handful to decorate and roughly chop the remainder and leave to cool slightly. Sift together **375g plain flour, 2 teaspoons baking powder, 1 teaspoon bicarbonate of soda** and **1/2 teaspoon ground cinnamon.** In another bowl whisk together **3 large organic eggs, 375ml groundnut or sunflower oil, 450g golden caster sugar** and **1 teaspoon vanilla extract** until smooth. Add the toasted walnuts, **500g coarsely grated carrots, 40g raisins, 100g desiccated coconut, 2 tablespoons of the juice from an orange and its zest** and mix until thoroughly combined. Stir in the sifted dry ingredients until smooth and divide the batter evenly between the prepared tins. Bake in the preheated oven for about 30-35 minutes or until a wooden skewer comes out clean when inserted into the middle of the cakes. Remove the cakes from the oven and leave to cool in the tins for 3-4 minutes and then turn out onto a wire cooling rack until completely cold. Beat together **50g unsalted softened butter** and **3 tablespoons honey or maple syrup** until combined. Add **300g cream cheese** and mix until smooth. Place 1 of the cake layers on a serving plate and spread with half of the cream cheese frosting. Top with the second cake and cover the top with the remaining cream cheese. Scatter with the reserved toasted walnuts to serve. Serves 8-10

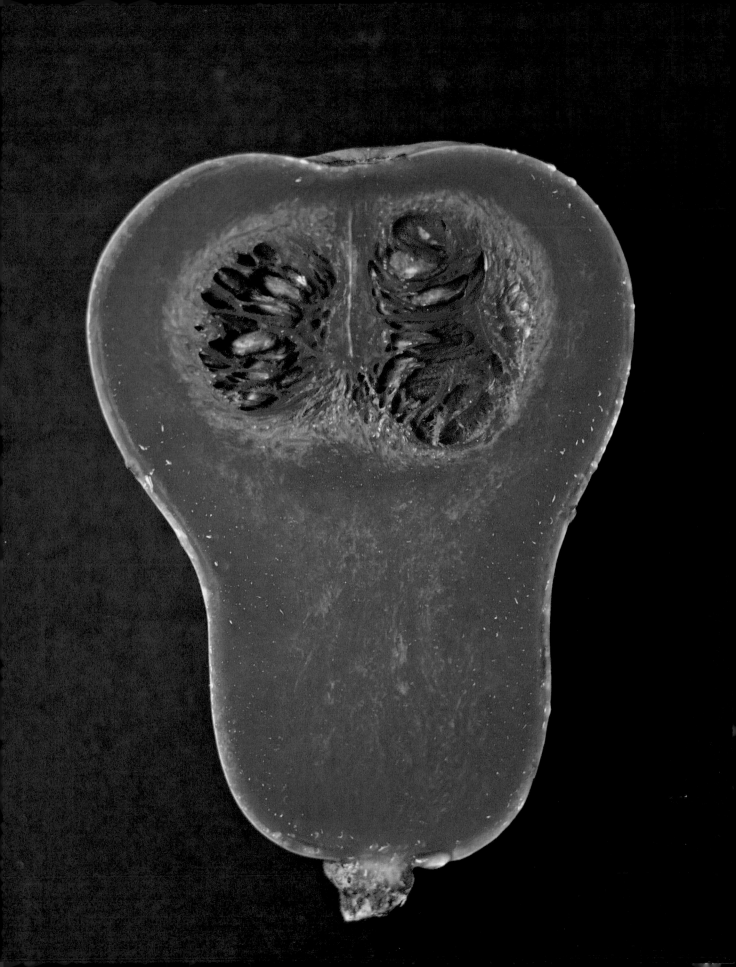

WEEK 11

BREAKFAST

ROASTED MUSHROOMS, TOMATOES AND PINE NUTS

Preheat the oven to 200°C/gas mark 6. Place **4 trimmed portobello mushrooms** on a baking tray, stalk side up. Season with **sea salt** and **freshly ground black pepper**. Drizzle with **1 tablespoon olive oil** and place in the oven for 10 minutes. After 5 minutes, add **100g cherry tomatoes on the vine** and return to the oven to continue cooking. Meanwhile toast **1 tablespoon pine nuts** in a dry frying pan, taking care not to burn them, and chop **1 tablespoon flatleaf parsley**. When the mushrooms are tender, remove from the oven, sprinkle with the pine nuts and parsley and serve the tomatoes on the side. Serves 2

PACKED LUNCH

SPICY BURRITO WITH SALSA AND GUACAMOLE

In a small bowl, mix **2 chopped spring onions** and **1/2 sliced red chilli** with some **salt** and **freshly ground black pepper** and set aside. Beat **4 organic eggs** and **100ml organic milk** with a fork with some salt and freshly ground black pepper. Heat **1 tablespoon olive oil** in a large non-stick pan and fry the spring onion and chilli for 1 minute, then pour in the egg mix. Gently scramble the eggs by dragging the egg mixture as it sets into the middle of the pan. Remove from the heat and mix in **a handful of freshly grated Cheddar**. Divide between **2 tortilla wraps**. Tuck up the top and bottom of each wrap and roll up, then slice in half and serve with **homemade tomato salsa** (see page 102), **soured cream** and **guacamole** (see page 102), if you wish. Serves 2

LUNCH

ROASTED BUTTERNUT SQUASH WITH PINE NUTS AND GOAT'S CHEESE

SERVES 2

Butternut squash is extremely tasty and the seeds can be eaten raw, fried or roasted. 'Squash' is an abbreviation of askuta squash, *the Native North American Indian word, and means 'eaten raw or uncooked'.*

1 small butternut squash
1 garlic clove, crushed
2 tablespoons olive oil
1 red chilli, deseeded and finely chopped
1 teaspoon fresh thyme leaves
100g goat's cheese, crumbled
50g pine nuts

Preheat the oven to 200°C/gas mark 6.

Cut the squash in half, scoop out the seeds, score the flesh with a sharp knife and place on a baking tray. In a bowl, mix together the garlic, olive oil, chilli and thyme and brush over the cut sides of the squash, pouring any excess into the wells left after deseeding. Place in the oven and bake for about 40 minutes until the flesh is tender and can be easily pierced with a fork.

Mix together the goat's cheese and pine nuts and spoon over the top of each of the squash halves. Return them to the oven and bake for a further 10 minutes until the cheese has melted and the pine nuts are lightly toasted.

SNACK

WHOLE ARTICHOKE WITH COBNUT DRESSING

OLIVER PEYTON

Bring a large pot of **salted water** to the boil. Cut **a lemon** in half and add it to the water. Break the stalks off **4 whole globe artichokes**. Boil in the salt water for 30 minutes, or until the outer leaves pull out easy. Stick a skewer into the core of the artichoke to check that the heart is tender. Remove from the pot to cool slightly and turned upside down to drain. Discard the centre leaves and the choke (fur) in the middle to make way for the vinaigrette. To make the vinaigrette, start by roasting **100g cobnuts** or **hazelnuts** in the oven until golden brown. Put them in the blender along with **25ml white wine vinegar** and **20g English mustard**, then add enough **olive oil** until you have the correct consistency for a vinaigrette and season to taste. Pour the vinaigrette into the centre of the artichoke. To eat, pull off the remaining leaves, dip the broken end into the vinaigrette and eat. Serves 4

DINNER

AUBERGINE, POTATO AND PEPPER STEW

SERVES 4

This rich, Mediterranean-inspired stew is full of flavours, which mature if there is any left over for the next day.

3 tablespoons olive oil
1 onion, chopped
1 stick celery, chopped
2 garlic cloves, crushed
1 red pepper, deseeded and cut into large chunks
1 medium courgette, cut into large chunks
1 aubergine, cut into large chunks
2 medium potatoes, peeled and cut into large chunks
1 teaspoon dried oregano
2 x 400g cans tomatoes
400ml vegetable stock
1 teaspoon caster sugar
400g can butterbeans, drained and rinsed
4 tablespoons kalamata olives
2 tablespoons toasted pine nuts
125g crumbled feta
2 tablespoons freshly chopped flatleaf parsley
salt and freshly ground black pepper

Heat half of the olive oil in a large casserole dish, add the chopped onion and celery and cook until tender but not coloured. Add the garlic and cook for a further minute. While the onion is cooking prepare the other vegetables.

Add the remaining oil, chopped peppers, courgette and aubergine to the pan and cook for 3–4 minutes. Add the potatoes, oregano, canned tomatoes and vegetable stock. Bring to the boil, season with salt and freshly ground black pepper, add the sugar, cover the pan and reduce the heat to a gentle simmer. Continue to cook for about 25–30 minutes until all of the veggies are tender. Add the butterbeans and olives and continue to cook for a further 5 minutes.

Check the seasoning, adding more salt and freshly ground black pepper if needed. Scatter with toasted pine nuts, crumbled feta and chopped parsley to serve.

DESSERT

LEMON DRIZZLE TRAYBAKE

Preheat the oven to 180°C/gas mark 4. Grease a 30 x 23cm baking tin. In a large bowl, beat together **200g butter** and **200g caster sugar** until light and fluffy. Beat in **3 organic eggs**, one at a time. Gently fold in **200g sifted self-raising flour**, then gently stir in **120ml organic milk** and the **grated zest of 2 lemons**. Spoon the mixture into the prepared tin, smooth the surface and bake for 30 minutes until golden. Using a skewer or cocktail stick, prick the cake all over. Mix together the **juice of the 2 lemons** with **100g granulated sugar**, and spoon over the cake. Leave to cool, then cut into squares. Makes 10 squares

WEEK 12

BREAKFAST

ONION AND WALNUT MUFFINS

Preheat the oven to 220°C /gas mark 7. Line two 12-hole muffin tins with muffin cases. Peel **1 large onion**, cut it into quarters and purée to achieve 250g. Beat together **250g butter, 2 organic eggs** and **6 tablespoons sugar** and add the onion purée. Stir in **1 teaspoon sea salt, 1 teaspoon baking powder, 300g shelled and coarsely crushed walnuts** and **350g plain flour** one by one and mix thoroughly. Fill the muffin tins almost full. Bake them for 20 minutes, or until they are puffed and well browned. Serve warm. Makes 20

PACKED LUNCH

PARSNIP SOUP

Heat **25g butter** and **1 tablespoon oil** in a large pan. Add **1 chopped onion, 1 peeled and chopped carrot** and **250g chopped parsnips** and cook gently for 5–6 minutes until softened but not browned. Add **750ml vegetable stock** and bring to the boil. Simmer for 25–30 minutes until the vegetables are soft. Purée the soup in a blender until smooth and return to the pan. You may have to do this in batches. Add **salt** and **freshly ground black pepper** to taste and serve hot with **a swirl of cream**, and **1 tablespoon freshly chopped parsley**. Serves 2–3

LUNCH

MUSHROOM, MASCARPONE AND POLENTA BAKE

KATIE CALDESI

SERVES 6

Polenta - basically cooked dough made from ground maize — was originally a peasant food. Now it regularly appears on the menus of chic restaurants. It's funny stuff. It can be stodgy if it isn't cooked properly, but well handled, as in this cheesy bake, it's delightful.

150g uncooked polenta,
*   or 600g cooked polenta*
salt
2 bay leaves
1 white onion (200g), sliced in rings
100g butter
300g mushrooms (mixed or one type only)

2 garlic cloves, finely chopped
2 sprigs of rosemary leaves
250g mascarpone
250g organic milk
a good pinch of grated nutmeg
200g vegetarian Parmesan
salt and freshly ground black pepper

Follow the cooking instructions on the packet for the uncooked polenta, using half water, half milk if desired, and adding salt and the bay leaves for extra flavour. Bring the liquid to the boil in a large saucepan, then whisk in the polenta. Keep stirring until all the polenta is incorporated, keeping it over a low heat for 40-45 minutes. Pour into a metal tray or glass dish and allow to cool and set. This will take 1-1 1/2 hours.

Preheat the oven to 180°C/gas mark 4. Fry the onion rings with a little salt and freshly ground black pepper in half the butter until soft. In another frying pan, fry the mushrooms, garlic and rosemary in the rest of the butter over a high heat, adding salt and freshly ground black pepper to taste. Meanwhile, mix the mascarpone and milk together with the nutmeg.

Cut the polenta into 0.5cm slices. Grease a medium ovenproof dish. Lay half the polenta slices in the base, scatter over the fried onions followed by the mushrooms, sprinkle with pepper and add half of the vegetarian Parmesan in a layer. Pour over half the mascarpone sauce and arrange the remaining polenta slices on top. Finish with the remaining sauce and top with the remaining Parmesan. Transfer the dish to the oven and bake for 30 minutes, or until bubbling and browned.

SNACK

HONEY-ROASTED NUTS AND SEEDS

Preheat the oven to 180°C/gas mark 4. Place **500g mixed nuts (almonds, brazil nuts, cashews, peanuts, pecans, walnuts), 50g pumpkin seeds** and **50g sunflower seeds** in a bowl. Pour over **2 tablespoons olive oil** and **2 tablespoons runny honey** and mix well so the nuts are evenly coated. Tip on to a large baking tray and spread out. Roast in the oven for 10 minutes, turning the nuts regularly so they brown evenly. When golden, remove from the oven and sprinkle with **1 teaspoon sea salt**. Serves 3-4

DINNER

BAKED PENNE WITH DOLCELATTE AND RADICCHIO

SERVES 4

Radicchio – a red form of chicory – is quite bitter when raw but cooking it mellows the flavour nicely. Some penne are smooth but the rigate kind have little ridges running along them. This allows sauces to cling to them, in this case a creamy mushroom and dolcelatte mixture.

250g penne rigate
50g butter
250g button mushrooms, halved
2 garlic cloves, finely chopped
1 tablespoon finely chopped fresh sage
1 small head of radicchio, cored and shredded finely

250ml double cream
50g vegetarian Parmesan, finely grated
175g dolcelatte, cubed
fresh sage leaves, to garnish
salt and freshly ground black pepper

Preheat the oven to 210°C/gas mark 7. Grease a 23 x 28cm ovenproof dish.

Cook the pasta in a large pan of boiling salted water, according to the packet instructions, until al dente, then drain.

Meanwhile, melt the butter in a large frying pan and fry the mushrooms and garlic for about 5 minutes until softened. Stir in the sage and radicchio and remove the pan from the heat. Season with salt and freshly ground pepper.

In a large bowl stir together the cream, half of the vegetarian Parmesan and dolcelatte. Add the mushroom mixture and pasta. Season to taste with salt and freshly ground black pepper. Spoon into the ovenproof dish, scatter with the remaining Parmesan and bake in the preheated oven for about 20 minutes until golden and bubbling. To serve, scatter over some fresh sage.

DESSERT

RHUBARB, APPLE AND OAT CRUMBLE

Preheat the oven to 200°C/gas mark 6. Peel, quarter and core **3 large Bramley apples** and cut into chunks. Slice **4-5 washed and trimmed sticks of rhubarb** and slice into similar size pieces to the apple. Tip the fruit into a large bowl, add **1/2 teaspoon ground cinnamon** and **2-3 tablespoons caster sugar** and mix well. Scoop the fruit into an ovenproof dish. Sift **250g plain flour** into another bowl and add **175g diced unsalted butter**. Rub the the butter into the flour until it resembles fine breadcrumbs. Add **75g golden (unrefined) granulated sugar**, **75g rolled oats** and **a pinch of salt** and mix thoroughly. Scatter the crumble evenly over the prepared fruit and place the dish on a baking tray. Cook the crumble on the middle shelf of the oven for 45 minutes or until the fruit is bubbling and the top is golden. Serve with **custard** or **double cream**. Serves 4-6

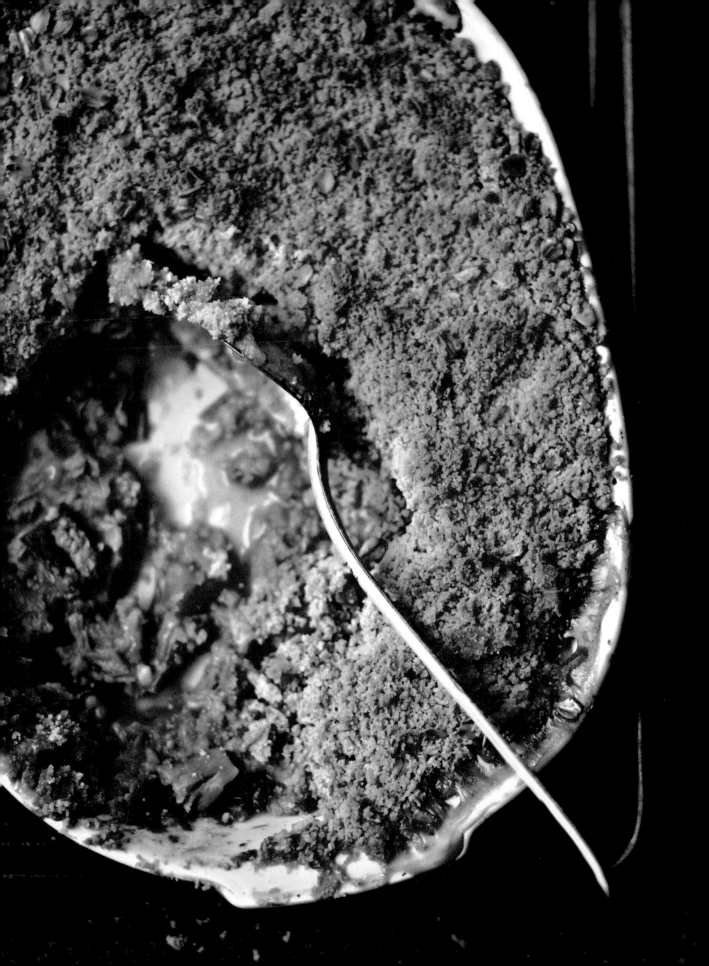

WEEK 13

BREAKFAST

WELSH RAREBIT

Preheat a grill and toast **4 large slices of bread** on one side. Mix together **25g softened butter, 1 teaspoon English mustard, salt** and **freshly ground black pepper, vegetarian Worcestershire sauce, 175g grated Cheddar** and **2 tablespoons organic milk**. Spread the mixture over the untoasted sides of the bread and brown under a hot grill for 2-3 minutes. Serve immediately. Serves 4

PACKED LUNCH

LEEK AND POTATO SOUP

Cut **3 large potatoes** into 1cm cubes and slice **1 leek** into 5mm rounds. Heat some **olive oil** in a saucepan over a medium heat, stir in the potato and leek and cook for 2 minutes. Add **750ml vegetable stock** and bring to the boil over a high heat. When it is boiling turn down the heat to low and simmer for 20 minutes. When the vegetables are cooked take the saucepan off the heat. With a ladle carefully place 3 ladlefuls of the soup in a liquidiser and blend for 10 seconds, then pour the blended soup into a big bowl. Repeat the blending until the saucepan is empty. Pour the blended soup back into the saucepan and reheat gently. Add **200ml semi-skimmed organic milk, salt** and **freshly ground black pepper** and simmer for 2 minutes more. Serves 4

LUNCH

SPICY TOFU WITH GINGER

JOSEPHINE FAIRLEY

SERVES 4

Tofu is very good at taking on the flavours of whatever it is marinated in. In this instance, it becomes infused with the enlivening taste of ginger. Tamari is a rich, dark variety of soy sauce.

*75g grated ginger
   (I use a Magimix for grating)*
5 garlic cloves, finely chopped
100ml tamari soy sauce
100ml olive oil
*350ml red or white wine (I use leftover wine
   rather than open something new)*
1 1/2 teaspoons turmeric
*50ml Rocks Ginger Cordial
   (you could also use ginger wine)*
900g firm tofu

TO SERVE
brown rice
salad
broccoli
organic sourdough bread

Put the grated ginger together with all the other ingredients apart from the tofu in a Magimix and whizz until smooth.

Cut the tofu into rectangular 2cm cubes. (The smaller the cube, the more the sauce gets into the middle of the tofu; however, too small and they'll become mushy when cooking.)

Pour the sauce over the cubed tofu in a lidded casserole, and leave to infuse in the fridge for anything between 4 to 24 hours. (The longer the better is my experience.)

Bake in the oven at 180°C/gas mark 4 for around 35 minutes; then remove the lid and cook for another 10 minutes.

Serve with brown rice and salad or green veg like broccoli. A good hunk of Judges organic sourdough bread (www.judgesbakery.com) also soaks up the sauce beautifully!

SIDE

ROASTED HERBY MUSHROOMS

Preheat the oven to 180°C/gas mark 4. Put **350g chestnut mushrooms** in a baking dish, stalk side up. Sprinkle over **1 teaspoon freshly chopped rosemary leaves, 1 teaspoon fresh thyme leaves, a pinch of sea salt** and **freshly ground black pepper**. Drizzle with **2 tablespoons olive oil** and **2 teaspoons lemon juice**. Bake for 30 minutes or until the mushrooms are tender. Serves 4

DINNER

PIZZA TWO WAYS

LAURA BAILEY

You are making two pizzas here, one topped with red onion and mozzarella, the other with butternut squash and feta. They make a lovely pair. You wouldn't call butternut squash a standard pizza topping but it turns out to be an inspired one.

FOR THE PIZZA DOUGH
300g strong flour
170ml water
1/2 teaspoon instant yeast
a large pinch of salt
1 tablespoon plain flour

FOR THE TOPPING
pesto
1/4 butternut squash, peeled and thinly sliced into crescent shapes
1 garlic clove, finely sliced olive oil
2 large red onions, cut into 24 wedges
2 tablespoons balsamic vinegar
40g soft brown sugar
100ml water
100g mozzarella
100g feta

SERVES 4

Preheat the oven to 180°C/gas mark 4.

To make the pizza dough add all the dry ingredients into the bowl of an electric mixer with the dough hook attachment. Slowly add the water. Allow the ingredients to combine and continue kneading the dough on a low speed for about 10 minutes. Leave the dough in the mixer bowl, cover it with clingfilm and leave in a warm place for about an hour.

Place the butternut squash and garlic into a baking dish. Drizzle with olive oil and sprinkle over some salt. Cook in the preheated oven for 15-20 minutes. When the squash is cooked remove from the oven and increase the heat to 200°C/gas mark 6.

Heat some olive oil in a saucepan, add the onions and allow to brown for about 5 minutes or so. Add the water, balsamic vinegar and soft brown sugar. Bring to the boil, put a lid on the saucepan and reduce the heat. Simmer until most of the liquid has evaporated. You should finish up with sweet, sticky, deep purple onions.

Divide the dough in two. Dust the work surface with flour and roll each one out to about 30-35cm rounds. They should be nice and thin. Place each pizza base on a baking tray.

Spread a fine layer of pesto on each base. On 1 base add the caramelised onion — you won't need all of it - then tear the mozzarella and place on the pizza. On the other base add the butternut squash and crumble on the feta. Season with a little salt and freshly ground black pepper and place in the oven for about 10-12 minutes. Serve with a handful of rocket on each and some toasted pine nuts on the butternut squash pizza.

DESSERT

VICTORIA SPONGE

Heat oven to 190°C/gas mark 5. Grease two 20cm cake tins and line with baking parchment. In a large bowl, beat **200g butter, 200g golden caster sugar, 4 organic eggs, 200g self-raising flour, 1 teaspoon baking powder** and **100ml organic milk** until you have a smooth batter. Divide the mixture between the tins, smooth the surface, then bake for about 20 minutes until golden. Turn onto a rack and leave to cool completely. To make the filling, beat **100g softened butter** until smooth, then gradually beat in **140g sifted icing sugar** and **1/2 teaspoon vanilla extract**. Spread over the bottom of 1 of the sponge layers, then top with **150g strawberry jam** and sandwich the second sponge on top. Dust with a little **icing sugar** before serving. Makes 8 slices

WIN

T

E

R

WEEK 01

BREAKFAST
CINNAMON CREPES

Mix **200g plain flour, 1 tablespoon baking powder** and **1 tablespoon caster sugar** then add **1 organic egg** and **275ml organic milk** until you have a thick batter. Rest the batter in the fridge for 30 minutes. Melt some **butter** in a non-stick pan, then drop in spoonfuls of the batter. When little holes appear in the surface, turn over and cook until golden on each side. Sprinkle with **ground cinnamon** and drizzle over some **runny honey,** if you wish. Serves 4

PACKED LUNCH
BLACK OLIVE, CHICORY AND ORANGE SALAD

Take **2 good chicory heads** and remove any damaged outer leaves before cutting them into slices about 1cm across. Make a dressing by mixing **3 tablespoons extra virgin olive oil** with **1 tablespoon white wine vinegar, salt** and **freshly ground black pepper,** and pour this over the chicory in a small bowl, tossing well. Peel and remove the pith from **1 large blood orange** and then divide into segments and cut each segment in 2. Add to the salad, along with **75g stoned black kalamata olives.** Toss well and serve. Serves 2

LUNCH
ALE AND PUFF PASTRY PIE

THE VEGETARIAN SOCIETY

SERVES 4

Being vegetarian, even if it's only for one day a week, doesn't mean you have to forsake the joys of ale-based pies. The light ale in this one does wondrous things to the chestnut mushrooms at its heart. It is also an incredibly easy pie to make.

100g margarine
2 large bunches spring onions, with the
    bottom 7cm chopped
550g small chestnut mushrooms, cut into
    5mm pieces
1 tablespoon cornflour
1/2 teaspoon yeast extract
300–350ml light ale
210g ready-rolled puff pastry
organic milk or soya milk

Preheat an oven to 200°C/gas mark 6.

Melt 50g margarine in a large non-stick frying pan. Sauté the chopped spring onions briefly. Add the chestnut mushrooms to the pan. Continue to sauté for 5 minutes until starting to colour, stirring to prevent sticking.

Remove from the heat and sprinkle with the cornflour. Once back on the hob, add the yeast extract and ale. Cook for a further 5 minutes or until the mushrooms begin to soften. Use more ale if the mixture seems too dry.

Divide the mixture into four small soufflé/ceramic pie dishes, then cut out four pastry circles to place on top, leaving some room to rise. Brush with milk or soya milk and make a small hole in the top to let the steam escape. Bake for 20 minutes until golden.

SIDE
PARSNIP GRATIN

Preheat the oven to 200°C/gas mark 6. To make the sauce melt **50g butter** in a saucepan, add **50g plain flour** and mix to a smooth paste. Cook for 2 minutes, stirring continuously. Remove the saucepan from the heat and gradually blend in **450ml organic milk**. Return to the heat and bring gently to the boil, stirring continuously until the sauce thickens. Stir in **5 tablespoons crème fraîche** and season with **salt** and **freshly ground black pepper**. Place **300g cooked parsnip chunks** in an ovenproof dish and pour over the sauce. Sprinkle **100g fresh breadcrumbs** and **2 tablespoons freshly grated vegetarian Parmesan** over the top and bake for 25–30 minutes or until the top is golden brown. Serves 4

DINNER
SPELT RISOTTO WITH BUTTERNUT SQUASH, SPINACH, CHESTNUTS AND GOAT'S CHEESE

SERVES 4

Spelt is an ancient form of wheat, tastier and more nutritious than its inbred cousins. Quite a lot of people with wheat intolerance are fine with it. This healthy 'risotto' is a great way to get acquainted with it.

1 butternut squash, peeled, deseeded and cut into chunks
8 sage leaves, chopped
4 garlic cloves, whole and lightly bruised
4 tablespoons olive oil
25g unsalted butter
4 shallots, chopped
250g pearled spelt

200ml dry white wine
750ml hot vegetable stock
2 handfuls of baby leaf spinach
10 chestnuts, cooked, peeled and roughly chopped
hard goat's cheese or pecorino
salt and freshly ground black pepper

Preheat the oven to 190°C/gas mark 5.

Tip the butternut squash into a roasting tin, add the chopped sage and whole, bruised garlic cloves, season and toss in 2–3 tablespoons of olive oil. Roast for about 25 minutes until tender and starting to brown at the edges.

Meanwhile start making the risotto. Heat the remaining oil and the butter in a large sauté pan over a medium heat. Add the chopped shallots and cook until tender but not coloured. Add the spelt and stir to coat in the shallots and butter. Continue to cook for 1 minute until the spelt starts to smell slightly nutty. Pour the white wine into the pan, stirring all the time. Allow most of the wine to evaporate and then add the stock a ladleful at a time stirring frequently until all of the stock has been absorbed and the spelt is tender.

Add the roasted butternut squash to the pan along with the baby leaf spinach and chestnuts. Stir to combine and season well with salt and freshly ground black pepper. Using a vegetable peeler shave the goat's cheese over the risotto and serve immediately.

DESSERT
CHOCOLATE MARZIPAN DATES

Pit **175g fresh dates** by scoring 1 side of the date and stuff with **50–75g marzipan**. Dip the dates in **75g melted dark chocolate** and roll in **25g chopped hazelnuts**. Place on a piece of baking parchment and chill in the refrigerator until set. Makes 12

WEEK 02

BREAKFAST

ENGLISH BREAKFAST MUFFINS

Dissolve **7g packet dried yeast** and **½ teaspoon sugar** in **a little tepid organic milk**. Sift **225g plain flour** into a bowl, add **a pinch of salt** and make a well in the centre. Pour in the yeast mixture and combine until it forms a dough. Cover the bowl and leave somewhere warm until the dough has doubled in size, about 30 minutes. Dust a work surface with flour and roll out the dough to a thickness of about 1cm. Cut into 8 rounds, each about 6–8cm in diameter. Place a non-stick pan on a very low heat and add **1 tablespoon oil**. Cook the muffins for 5–7 minutes on each side until lightly golden brown. To serve, allow to cool slightly, then split in half and lightly toast. Makes 8

PACKED LUNCH

CURRIED EGG, ALMOND AND BROWN RICE

Cook **250g long grain brown rice** in lightly salted water for 30–35 minutes or until just tender. Drain, run under cold water and drain again. Heat **4 tablespoons sunflower oil** in a wok or large frying pan over a high heat. Shred **1 small cabbage** and add it to the wok or pan with **1 finely chopped garlic clove** and stir-fry for 3 minutes or until the cabbage begins to soften. Stir in **125g shelled almonds**, the rice, **1 teaspoon Madras curry powder** and **1 teaspoon ground turmeric** and cook for a further 2 minutes. Chop and mix in **6 hard-boiled organic eggs**. Serves 4

LUNCH

BEETROOT, RED ONION AND CHICORY SALAD

STELLA McCARTNEY

SERVES 4

Endive is grown in the dark to produce tight, pale heads that are bitter but in a good way. The pears and feta in this recipe take the edge off it, as does the beetroot.

1 bunch (about 5) golfball-size beetroot, trimmed of stalk and leaves
3 tablespoons olive oil
1 tablespoon red wine vinegar
100g pecans
2 tablespoons clear honey
2 red onions, chopped into wedges
3 garlic cloves, whole and unpeeled
2 ripe pears, quartered, cored and sliced
2 heads chicory, trimmed into separate leaves

large handful of wild rocket
150g feta, crumbled

FOR THE DRESSING
3 tablespoons walnut oil
juice of ½ lemon
1 rounded teaspoon Dijon mustard
salt and freshly ground black pepper

Preheat the oven to 180°C/gas mark 4. Lay a large piece of foil in a small roasting tin, tip the beets into the middle, season and drizzle with half of the olive oil and the red wine vinegar. Wrap the foil over and seal tightly. Roast the beetroot for 1 hour or until tender when tested with the point of a sharp knife. Remove from the roasting tin and leave to cool.

Tip the pecans into the roasting tin and drizzle with the honey. Stir to coat then roast for about 10 minutes until sticky and glazed. Remove from the roasting tin and cool the nuts on a plate.

Tip the onions into a baking tray, add the garlic cloves, drizzle with the remaining olive oil and roast for about 30 minutes until tender and starting to caramelise.

To make the dressing, squeeze the roasted garlic cloves from their skins into a small bowl, add the remaining ingredients and gently whisk until just combined. Peel the beets and cut into wedges. In a large serving bowl layer the beetroot, onion, pears, chicory, wild rocket, crumbled feta and honey roast pecans. Generously drizzle with the dressing and serve immediately.

SIDE

ROASTED ACORN SQUASH

Preheat the oven to 180°C/gas mark 4. Allow **100g acorn squash** per person. Cut in half and remove the seeds and fibres. Place in a greased ovenproof dish and pour over **1 tablespoon balsamic vinegar, 2 tablespoons runny honey** and **1 tablespoon lemon juice** for each serving. Cook in the oven for 40 minutes until tender, turning over halfway. Serves 2

DINNER

LEEK AND RICOTTA TART

The French for leek is 'poireau', which is related to the word for pears (poires). The two come from very different families but there's definitely a connection in their sweet softness when cooked. The combination of pine nuts and raisins with leeks may well be new to you but it's certainly a successful one.

4 largish leeks, trimmed and roughly chopped
2 tablespoons olive oil
2 garlic cloves, finely chopped
225g ricotta
2 tablespoons toasted pine nuts
3 tablespoons raisins, softened in warm water
1 organic egg
salt and freshly ground black pepper

FOR THE PASTRY
90g butter
175g plain flour
3 tablespoons water
pinch of salt

SERVES 4

Make the pastry by crumbling the butter into the flour and then adding water to make a dough. Add the salt and sprinkle with flour. Wrap in clingfilm and chill in the fridge for 30 minutes.

Preheat the oven to 190°C/gas mark 5.

Steam the leeks gently for about 10 minutes and drain. In a heavy-bottomed frying pan heat the oil and gently fry the garlic. Then add the leeks and stir to coat well with oil; allow them to cook for about 5 minutes, stirring occasionally.

Remove from the heat. In a bowl mix the ricotta with the pine nuts and raisins, and bind with the egg. Add the leeks, mix well and season then set aside to cool. Gently roll out the pastry to fit a 20cm tart tin. Prick the base and bake blind for 10–15 minutes. Fill the tart with the leek and ricotta mixture and return to the oven to cook for a further 30 minutes or until risen and golden.

DESSERT

EASY CHOCOLATE FUDGE PUDDING

Preheat the oven to 180°C/gas mark 4. Grease a 1 litre baking dish. Sift **100g plain flour** into a mixing bowl and add **1 teaspoon baking powder, 2 tablespoons cocoa** and **100g golden caster sugar**. Make a well in the centre, pour in **100g melted butter, 2 organic eggs, 1 teaspoon vanilla extract** and **1–2 tablespoons organic milk,** and beat until well combined. Stir in **50g chopped pecans,** and pour into the prepared tin. In another bowl, combine **100g soft brown sugar, 2 tablespoons cocoa** and **120ml hot water**. Stir well and pour over the cake batter. Place in the oven and bake for 40 minutes. During baking the cake will rise to the top and underneath there will be a delicious chocolate sauce. Serve hot with **cream**. Serves 4

WEEK 03

BREAKFAST
HASH BROWNS

Grate **1 large unpeeled potato** onto a clean tea towel. Bring up the edges of the towel, then squeeze over the sink to remove any excess water in the potatoes. Tip into a bowl and add **1 tablespoon plain flour** and **1 tablespoon Dijon mustard**. Season with **salt** and **freshly ground black pepper** and mix together. Divide the mixture into 8 balls and flatten between your hands. Heat a large frying pan with **25g butter** and **1 tablespoon sunflower oil**, then add the potato patties to the pan. Cook for 2–3 minutes on each side, over a medium heat, until golden. Stack a couple of hash browns on each serving plate and top with **a freshly poached organic egg** or **a couple of dollops of crème fraîche**. Serves 4

PACKED LUNCH
PAPPARDELLE WITH CAVOLO NERO

Heat a large saucepan of salted water and bring to the boil. Add **125g pappardelle** and cook for 6–8 minutes, until al dente. Meanwhile, heat **1 tablespoon olive oil** in a medium saucepan and, when hot, add **2 finely chopped garlic cloves**. Add **100g roughly chopped cavolo nero (stalks removed)** and stir to wilt in the oil. Season with **salt** and **freshly ground black pepper**. Add **75ml white wine** and boil for 2–3 minutes until reduced. Add **2 tablespoons crème fraîche** and **2 tablespoons freshly grated vegetarian Parmesan** and heat through. Drain the pasta, stir into the sauce and serve immediately with some **extra Parmesan** in a bowl. Serves 2

LUNCH
JERUSALEM ARTICHOKE SOUP

Not to be confused with Globe Artichokes, which are another kettle of fish entirely, the Jerusalem kind are the tubers of a member of the sunflower family. They are nutty and earthy and full of flavour.

500g Jerusalem artichokes
2 tablespoons olive oil
2 large onions, chopped
1 large garlic clove, crushed
600ml vegetable stock
strip of orange peel
4 tablespoons thick cream
salt and freshly ground black pepper

SERVES 4

Scrub the artichokes, discard any hard knobs and roughly chop. Heat the oil in a heavy-bottomed pan and add the onions. Cook until translucent, add the garlic, continue cooking for a couple of minutes and add the artichokes. Toss well to coat with oil and pour in the vegetable stock. Bring to the boil, add the orange peel and season with salt and freshly ground black pepper. Cover and simmer for 15–20 minutes, until cooked. Remove from the heat, discard the peel and blend in a food-processor. Return to the pan, adjust the seasoning, stir in the cream and serve.

SIDE

WINTER COLESLAW

VIVIENNE WESTWOOD

Cut **1 small white cabbage** in half, finely shred and put in a large bowl. Add **1 thinly sliced red onion** and **1 coarsely grated carrot** and mix well. In a separate bowl, whisk together **3 tablespoons good-quality mayonnaise, 1 tablespoon cider vinegar** and **1 tablespoon runny honey**, then stir in **2 teaspoons toasted caraway seeds**. Stir the dressing into the cabbage mix and chill for at least an hour. Serves 4

DINNER

LENTIL, CHICKPEA, CHEDDAR AND ONION BURGERS

SERVES 4

Guilt-free fast food! Perfect in a toasted bun, these deliciously spicy burgers will become firm family favourites and are guaranteed to convert even the most committed of carnivores.

3 tablespoons olive oil
1 large onion, chopped
2 cloves garlic, crushed
1 teaspoon ground cumin
1/4 teaspoon cayenne pepper
400g can lentils, drained and rinsed
400g can chickpeas, drained and rinsed
1 tablespoon tahini paste
2 tablespoons freshly chopped parsley
1 large organic egg, beaten
100g fresh breadcrumbs
100g grated Gruyère
100g feta, crumbled
plain flour, for dusting
salt and freshly ground black pepper

TO SERVE
burger buns
shredded lettuce
sliced tomatoes
sliced red onions
sliced avocados
soured cream
tomato ketchup
mayonnaise
pickles and relishes

Heat 1 tablespoon of olive oil in a frying pan, add the chopped onion and cook over a medium heat until tender but not coloured. Add the garlic, ground cumin and cayenne and cook for another 30 seconds. Remove from the heat.

Tip the lentils and chickpeas into the bowl of a food-processor and blend until coarsely chopped. Add the onion mixture, tahini paste and parsley, and blend again until combined and nearly smooth. Tip into a large bowl and add the beaten egg, breadcrumbs and both of the cheeses. Mix together using your hands and season well with salt and freshly ground black pepper.

Shape the mixture into patties and lightly dust in plain flour. Heat the remaining olive oil in a large frying pan, slide the burgers into the pan and cook until golden on both sides.

Serve in toasted buns with lettuce, tomatoes, onions and avocados and a dollop of soured cream, ketchup or mayonnaise and pickles of your choice.

DESSERT

CAPPUCCINO CUPCAKES

Preheat the oven to 180°C/gas mark 4. Line a 12-hole muffin tin with muffin cases. In a large mixing bowl, cream **75g unsalted butter** and **150g soft light brown sugar** together until pale and creamy. Add **2 organic eggs** one at a time, mixing all the time. The mixture might look split at this stage but, don't worry, that's normal. Sift **85g plain flour** and **85g self-raising flour** together into a bowl. Mix **1 tablespoon instant espresso powder** and **90ml organic milk** together in a separate bowl. Fold in one third of the flour mixture and beat well then half of the coffee mixture and beat well again. Repeat the process, beating well between each addition. Spoon the mixture into the muffin cases until two thirds full. Bake for 20–25 minutes until golden brown and springy to the touch. Transfer to a wire rack to cool. For the topping, whisk **300ml whipping cream** and **25g icing sugar** together to soft peaks. Spoon the cream into a piping bag fitted with a star nozzle and pipe swirls over the cupcakes. Decorate each cupcake with a **chocolate-covered espresso bean** and dust with **drinking chocolate powder**. Makes 12

WEEK 04

BREAKFAST

CLASSIC IRISH SODA BREAD

This is delicious served warm, spread with butter and jam. Preheat the oven to 190°C/gas mark 5 and dust a baking tray with flour. Sift **250g plain flour, 250g wholemeal flour, 2 teaspoons bicarbonate of soda** and **a pinch of salt** into a large bowl. Rub in **25g butter**. Make a well in the centre and pour in **400ml buttermilk**, and stir it quickly into the dry ingredients using a knife. If the dough seems too dry, add a little more buttermilk. Bring the dough gently together using your hands and shape into a ball roughly 20cm in diameter. Place on the baking tray and make two deep incisions across the top using a sharp serrated knife. Bake in the oven for 35–40 minutes. When done, the loaf should sound hollow when tapped on the bottom. Transfer to a wire rack to cool, covering it with a cloth to keep the crust soft. Any bread that isn't eaten fresh can be toasted the next day. Serves 4

PACKED LUNCH

PUMPKIN SOUP

Heat oven to 200°C/gas mark 6. Peel and cut **1kg pumpkin** into large cubes, about 4cm across, then toss in a large roasting tin with **1 tablespoon olive oil**. Roast for 30 minutes, turning once during cooking, until golden and soft. While the pumpkin cooks, melt **1 tablespoon butter** with **1 tablespoon olive oil** in a large saucepan, then add **2 diced onions, 1 thinly sliced garlic clove, 2 tablespoons coarsely chopped ginger** and **2 finely chopped red chillies**. Cover and cook on a very low heat for 15–20 minutes until the onions are completely soft. Tip the pumpkin into the pan, add **850ml hot vegetable stock** and **4 tablespoons crème fraîche**, then whizz with a stick blender until smooth. Return to the pan, gently reheat, then season to taste with **salt** and **freshly ground black pepper**. Serve the soup in bowls with swirls of **crème fraîche**. Serves 6

LUNCH

MISO BROTH

Miso is a wonderful savoury substance made by fermenting soya beans with wheat, barley or rye. Miso soup is practically Japan's national dish.

2 teaspoons sesame oil
200g mushrooms (enoki or shiitake), sliced
½ carrot, peeled and sliced into matchsticks
1 red chilli, sliced
1 tablespoon shredded fresh ginger
good handful of choi sum or baby leaf spinach, shredded

5 spring onions, trimmed and finely sliced on the diagonal
2 tablespoons yellow miso paste
125g tofu, drained and cut into small dice
tamari or soy sauce to taste

SERVES 2

Heat the sesame oil in a wok or large frying pan and add the mushrooms and carrots. Quickly cook the veggies for a minute until just softened then add the chilli and ginger and cook for another 10 seconds.

Throw the choi sum or baby leaf spinach and spring onions into the wok and cook until the leaves are only just wilted. Remove from the pan and divide between 2 bowls.

Bring 700ml water to the boil in a large pan. In a small bowl mix the miso with a couple of tablespoons of the water and then add the paste to the pan. Stir to combine and add a little more miso if needed. Divide the drained and diced tofu between the bowls and pour over the miso broth. Add tamari or soy sauce to taste and serve immediately.

SIDE

BUBBLE AND SQUEAK

Mash **500g peeled and boiled floury potatoes** with **50g butter** and season with **salt** and **freshly ground black pepper**. Crumble **250g cabbage or Brussels sprouts** into the mash with **1 tablespoon freshly chopped parsley**. Shape the potato mix into 4 rounds and flatten slightly with the palm of your hand. Heat **3 tablespoons oil** in a frying pan and fry the cakes for 4 minutes on each side, or until golden. Serve with **roasted vine** or **cherry tomatoes** and **tomato chutney**. Serves 4

DINNER

VEGETABLE PUFF PIE

SERVES 4

This classically British pie cries out for mashed potato as an accompaniment. You'll certainly want something to mop up the juices.

50g butter, plus 1 tablespoon
40g plain flour, plus extra for dusting
450ml organic milk
125g grated Cheddar
1 tablespoon freshly chopped parsley
1 teaspoon English mustard powder
1 carrot, thinly sliced

125g button mushrooms, halved
1 leek, trimmed and finely sliced
200g broccoli, chopped into small florets
250g ready-to-roll puff pastry
1 beaten organic egg to glaze
1 tablespoon sesame seeds
salt and freshly ground black pepper

Preheat the oven to 200°C/gas mark 6.

Melt 50g butter in a saucepan, add the flour and cook for 1 minute. Remove from the heat and gradually whisk in the milk. Return to the heat and bring to the boil, stirring continuously until the sauce thickens. Stir in the cheese, parsley and mustard powder.

In another pan, heat the remaining butter, add the carrots and the mushrooms and cook until tender. Meanwhile, cook the leek for 5 minutes in a pan of salted boiling water and then add the broccoli and cook until tender. Drain.

Combine the vegetables with the sauce, mix well, and place the mixture in a lightly-greased large pie dish.

Dampen the pie dish rim. Roll out the pastry on a lightly-floured work surface. Cut off a strip of pastry and place it on the rim of the dish and brush it with water.

Lay the pastry lid over the top and press the edges together to seal. Trim and flute the edges. Make a hole in the top of the pie to let out the air whilst cooking and use the trimmings to decorate the pie. Glaze with the beaten egg and sprinkle with sesame seeds.

Cook in the preheated oven for 30 minutes until golden brown.

DESSERT

CHOCOLATE BREAD AND BUTTER PUDDING

Preheat the oven to 190°C /gas mark 5. You will need an ovenproof dish 18cm long and 4cm deep. In a medium size saucepan bring **600ml organic milk** and **284ml double cream** to the boil over a moderate heat. Meanwhile mix together in a bowl **4 organic egg yolks** and **125g caster sugar**. Pour over the organic milk and cream mixture, stir well to combine, then strain into a jug, adding **a few drops of vanilla extract**. Layer **¼ sliced baguette** in the bottom of the ovenproof dish, and scatter over **50g sultanas** and **50g roughly chopped plain chocolate**. Dip **¼ sliced baguette** in **50g melted butter** and lay the sliced on top of the sultanas. Pour over the custard mixture and leave to soak for 30 minutes, pushing the bread beneath the surface of the custard. Place the dish in a bain-marie (a roasting tin containing boiling hot water to reach to halfway up the sides of the ovenproof dish). Bake the pudding for 1 hour until golden brown. In a small saucepan heat together **4 tablespoons apricot jam** and **2 tablespoons orange juice**. Brush liberally over the bread and butter pudding and serve immediately. Serves 4–6

WEEK 05

BREAKFAST
GRANOLA

Preheat the oven to 180°C/gas mark 4. Roughly chop **200g mixed nuts such as almonds, pecans and hazelnuts** and tip into a large bowl. Add **450g rolled oats, 50g sunflower seeds, 50g pumpkin seeds, 50g linseeds and 50g desiccated coconut** and mix well. Add **125ml sunflower oil** and **100ml runny honey** and mix thoroughly to combine. Pour the mixture into a large roasting tin and spread into an even layer. Bake for 20 minutes or until golden and crisp, stirring frequently so that the mixture toasts evenly. Remove from the oven and add **100g roughly chopped dried cherries, cranberries or blueberries**. Leave to cool before scooping into storage jars. Serve with **fresh berries**, **organic milk** or **natural yogurt**. Makes 12 servings

PACKED LUNCH
CHEESE AND ONION SANDWICH

Mix together **40g soft goat's cheese** with **20g cream cheese**. Heat a little **olive oil** in a pan and add **half a sliced red onion**. Allow the onion to sweat. When it starts to wilt, add **¼ teaspoon sugar, a pinch of salt**, some **freshly ground black pepper** and **1 teaspoon balsamic vinegar**. Cook for a further 3–4 minutes. Spread the goat's cheese mixture over a slice of **granary bread** and top with the red onion and **a handful of rocket leaves**. Place another slice of granary bread on top and season with **salt** and **freshly ground black pepper**. Serves 1

LUNCH
CHICKPEA CURRY

SKYE GYNGELL

SERVES 4

Chickpeas are high in protein. Soaking them overnight reduces the cooking time, while the bicarbonate of soda in this recipe helps soften them.

600g dried chickpeas, soaked overnight
1 teaspoon bicarbonate of soda
1 teaspoon mustard seeds
1 teaspoon fennel seeds
1 teaspoon cumin seeds
1 teaspoon coriander seeds
5 cardamom pods
1 tablespoon vegetable oil
2 red onions, sliced

1 small bunch of coriander, roots included
1 red chilli
3 garlic cloves, chopped
4 carrots, peeled and diced
3 tablespoons maple syrup
juice of 2 limes
3 tablespoons soy sauce
2 jars of good-quality tomatoes
50g unsalted butter

Drain and place the chickpeas in a large pot of cold water. Add a teaspoon of bicarbonate of soda. Cook over a medium heat for around 45 minutes or until tender. Drain and set aside.

To make the base of the curry, warm up the spices in a small pan, being careful not to burn them, as this will result in a bitter taste. Grind using a pestle and mortar. Add the vegetable oil to a pot large enough to hold all the ingredients comfortably and place over a medium heat. When the oil is warm, add the onions and soften for 5 minutes. Chop the coriander and the chilli very finely and add to the pot along with the garlic and the spices.

Add the diced carrots and cook for 10 minutes. Then add the maple syrup, lime juice and soy sauce, stirring well to combine the flavours, and cook for another few minutes. Add the tomatoes and turn up the heat slightly. Cook for 15 minutes to thicken the sauce. At this point it should taste hot, sweet and slightly sharp. Keep the pan over the heat until the carrots are cooked through but still firm. At this point, add the chickpeas and the butter and serve.

SIDE

POTATOES WITH HAZELNUTS AND ROSEMARY

SIMON ROGAN

Take about **15g tiny rosemary needles** from the bunch and set aside. Boil **450g pink fir potatoes** with **25g sprig of rosemary leaves**. Meanwhile simmer **25g hazelnuts** in water for 4 minutes, drain, peel and pat dry. Gently fry the hazelnuts in **a little hazelnut oil** until golden brown, season with **salt** and **freshly ground black pepper**, cool down and crush into smaller pieces. When the potatoes are cooked, peel, slice and fry in a generous amount of hazelnut oil until they are golden brown. Remove and drain onto kitchen paper, wipe clean the pan and place in to it another **2 tablespoons of hazelnut oil** with **100ml crème fraîche**. Reduce until the sauce is the right consistency, add the rosemary needles and return the golden potato slices. Season with **salt** and **freshly ground black pepper**, place into a bowl and scatter over the fried hazelnut pieces. Serves 4

DINNER

ROASTED VEG AND MISO DRESSING WITH SESAME SEEDS

SERVES 4

Miso is rich in what the Japanese call umami — a lip-smacking savoury tang often described as the fifth fundamental flavour (the others are sweet, salt, sour and bitter). It's used to make a tasty Miso Broth on page 189; today you're going to exploit one of miso's other virtues — it's great in salad and vegetable dressings.

3 medium size carrots, peeled and cut in half lengthways
1 butternut squash, peeled, deseeded and cut into wedges
3 small-medium parsnips, peeled and halved (or quartered if they are large)
2 tablespoons olive oil
200g tenderstem broccoli, trimmed
2 tablespoons runny honey
1 tablespoon mixed black and white sesame seeds

FOR THE DRESSING
3 tablespoons toasted sesame oil
2 teaspoons freshly grated ginger
1 garlic clove, crushed
1 heaped teaspoon yellow miso paste
1 tablespoon rice vinegar

Preheat the oven to 190°C/gas mark 5.

Prepare the vegetables, then tip the carrots, squash and parsnips into a large bowl and toss with 1–2 tablespoons olive oil. Arrange the veggies in a roasting tin in a single layer and cook on the middle shelf of the preheated oven for about 25 minutes or until tender and starting to brown at the edges. Add the broccoli to the tin, drizzle the vegetables with 1 tablespoon of the honey and scatter over the sesame seeds. Return to the oven and continue to cook for a further 5 minutes to caramelise.

While the vegetables are cooking prepare the dressing. Spoon the remaining tablespoon of honey into a small bowl, add the other dressing ingredients and whisk lightly to combine. Arrange the warm honey-roasted vegetables on a platter, drizzle with the dressing and serve.

DESSERT

PECAN PIE

Lightly flour a work surface and roll out **500g shortcrust pastry** to a thickness of 3–4mm. Line a 23cm pie dish with the pastry and trim the excess, leaving a 2.5cm overhang. Using your fingers, take the overhang and roll it under itself allowing the rolled edge to rest on the edge of the pie dish. Crimp the edge with your fingers, then chill for 30 minutes or until firm. Preheat the oven to 180°C/gas mark 4. Line the prepared pastry with baking parchment and a layer of baking beans and bake for 15 minutes. Remove the parchment and beans and bake for a further 10 minutes or until the pie begins to turn golden in colour. Meanwhile, make the filling by whisking together **70g melted butter, 200g dark brown sugar, 350g golden syrup, 4 organic eggs, 1 teaspoon vanilla extract** and **¼ teaspoon salt** in a medium bowl. Scatter the pie base with **150g chopped pecan nuts**, pour over the filling and top with another **50g chopped pecans**. Bake in the oven for 50 minutes – 1 hour or until the filling is set. Allow to cool before serving. Serves 8–10

WEEK 06

BREAKFAST
POTATO FARLS

Cut **1 medium size floury potato** into chunks and cook in boiling water until tender. Drain well and press through a potato ricer or mash. Weigh out 125g and cool. Sieve **35g plain flour** and **1/2 teaspoon baking powder** onto the cooled mash. Whisk **1 organic egg** and **60ml organic milk** together and add to the potato mix. Whisk the batter until smooth. Heat a large non-stick frying pan over a medium heat. Add **1/2 teaspoon sunflower oil** and **a dot of butter**. Add **1 tablespoon of batter** for each farl and cook 4 at a time. Cook for about 1 minute until the underside is golden brown and small bubbles appear. Flip the farls and cook until golden. Remove from the pan and keep warm while you cook the remaining farls in the same way, adding a tiny bit of oil and butter to the pan as and when needed. Serve with **grated mature Cheddar** or crumble over some **vegetarian blue cheese** and drizzle with **honey**. Makes 6–8

PACKED LUNCH
PILAU RICE WITH CASHEWS

Heat **2 tablespoons oil** in a large saucepan, add **4 finely chopped shallots** and cook for 5 minutes, stirring occasionally, without browning. Stir in **1 teaspoon ground cumin, 1 teaspoon ground coriander, 1/2 teaspoon chilli powder, 6 cardamom pods, 2.5cm of cinnamon stick, 1 blade mace** and cook for 2 minutes, ensuring that they do not burn. Add **2 crushed garlic cloves** and **250g basmati rice** and cook for 5 minutes, stirring constantly. Pour in **600ml vegetable stock**, season with **salt**, cover and simmer for 15 minutes, stirring occasionally, until the rice is tender and the stock has been absorbed. Transfer to a warmed serving plate, sprinkle with **50g roasted cashew nuts** and garnish with **a handful of coriander leaves**. Serves 3–4

LUNCH
CAULIFLOWER KORMA

As any fan of Indian cookery knows, korma is a mild, creamy kind of curry. Cauliflower and Brazil nuts share those qualities, making for a fantastic, simple to prepare lunch.

3 tablespoons vegetable oil
1 medium onion, sliced
1 garlic clove, crushed
1 red chilli, deseeded and finely chopped
2 teaspoons medium hot curry powder
100g Brazil nut kernels

75g creamed coconut made up to 450ml with water
1 small cauliflower, cut into small florets
125g broccoli, cut into small florets
2 courgettes, cut into small chunks

SERVES 4

Heat the oil in a frying pan and fry the onion, garlic, chilli and curry powder for 5 minutes.

Purée half the Brazil nut kernels in a food-processor then add them to the coconut liquid and pour the liquid into the frying pan. Combine and remove from the heat.

Bring a pan of water to the boil and parboil the vegetables: boil the cauliflower for 3 minutes, the broccoli for 2 minutes and the courgettes for 1 minute. Drain.

Add all the vegetables to the korma sauce and simmer for 4 minutes, stirring in the remaining Brazil nut kernels just before serving.

SIDE

SPICY BEETROOT SALAD

Cook **750g trimmed beetroots** in a steamer for 20–30 minutes until tender. Peel and slice them when cool, reserving the liquid that accumulates on the plate. Toss them in the **juice of 1/2 lemon** and coat with **1/2 teaspoon ground cumin, 1/2 teaspoon ground cinnamon, 1/2 teaspoon ground paprika, 1 tablespoon orange flower water** and **2 tablespoons olive oil**, together with the liquid. Season with **salt** and **freshly ground black pepper**, cover and chill. To serve, toss with **2 tablespoons freshly chopped parsley** and arrange on individual plates on a bed of **mixed lettuce leaves** — coloured varieties mixed with green leaves such as lamb's lettuce work well. Serves 4

DINNER

VEGETABLE AND TOFU STIR-FRY WITH SOBA NOODLES

SERVES 4

Soba is the Japanese name for buckwheat noodles, which are thin and brown, and tastier and more substantial than most other kinds. This fresh, crunchy stir-fry shows them off to good advantage.

1/2 head Chinese leaves, cut into 1cm ribbons
100g shiitake mushrooms, halved
1 bunch spring onions, cut into 5cm lengths
100g baby corn, sliced in half
100g mangetout, sliced in half
250g firm tofu, drained and cut into
    2cm cubes
250g soba noodles

1 tablespoon toasted sesame oil
1 tablespoon soy sauce
4 tablespoons vegetable oil
2 tablespoons rice flour
1 garlic clove, crushed
100g beansprouts
2 tablespoons shoyo (Japanese soy sauce)
fresh chives to garnish (optional)

Prepare the vegetables and set them aside in small piles.

Bring a large saucepan of water to the boil and cook the noodles according to the instructions on the pack, until just tender. Drain well and toss in the sesame oil and soy sauce.

Meanwhile, heat half the oil in a wok or large frying pan, dust the tofu cubes in rice flour and fry in the hot oil until golden. Remove from the pan. Add the remaining oil to the wok, add the garlic and fry for a few seconds and then add the mushrooms, spring onions and baby corn. Stir fry over a high heat for 3 minutes.

Add the Chinese leaves, beansprouts and mangetout, and sprinkle in the shoyo. Continue to stir-fry for a further 2–3 minutes until the vegetables are just tender. Return the tofu to the pan and stir to combine and heat through.

To serve, divide the noodles between 4 warmed serving plates and top with the stir-fried vegetables. Garnish with chives, if desired.

DESSERT

CHOCOLATE TRUFFLES

This recipe uses raw egg, which should be avoided by the elderly and very young. Melt **175g plain chocolate** in a bowl over a pan of hot water. Add **1 organic egg yolk, 25g butter** and **1 teaspoon coffee essence** and leave in a cool place for 30–40 minutes until set. Mould into small egg shapes with your fingers and roll in **1 tablespoon cocoa** to coat evenly. Makes 20

WEEK 07

BREAKFAST

CHOCOLATE CROISSANT

Heat oven to 180°C/gas mark 4. Slice **1 croissant** in half lengthways, but don't go all the way through – it should open like a book. Sprinkle the bottom half of the croissant with **1 tablespoon chopped milk chocolate**. Close up, put on a baking tray and grate **a little chocolate** over top. Bake in the oven for 5 minutes or until the chocolate has melted. Serve warm. Serves 1

PACKED LUNCH

WENSLEYDALE AND CARROT CHUTNEY SANDWICH

The chutney will need to be made in advance but is well worth it. In a bowl, mix together **500g grated carrot, 1 teaspoon grated ginger, 250ml cider vinegar, 1 finely chopped red chilli, 1 teaspoon crushed fennel seeds** and **a pinch of salt**. Cover and set aside for 24 hours. Pour the mixture into a pan, add **100ml water** and bring to the boil, then reduce the heat to low and simmer for 10 minutes. Stir in **350g brown sugar**, increase the heat and then boil the mixture until it becomes thick, about 30 minutes. Remove from the heat and spoon into sterilised jars. To make your sandwich, take **2 slices of granary bread** and spread with butter. Crumble **50g Wensleydale cheese** over one of the buttered slices, then spread with 1 tablespoon of the carrot chutney. Top with **a handful of rocket leaves** and the remaining slice of bread. Serves 1

LUNCH

ONION BHAJIS WITH TOMATO AND CHILLI SAUCE

DARINA ALLEN

SERVES 4

Onion bhajis are very popular in Britain but shop-bought ones can be greasy and tired. These ones are anything but. They are served with a feisty sauce that transforms what is usually thought of as a snack into a satisfying meal.

FOR THE TOMATO AND CHILLI SAUCE
25g green chillies, deseeded and chopped
1 red pepper, deseeded and cut in 5mm dice
1/2 x 400g can of chopped tomatoes
1 garlic clove, crushed
1 teaspoon caster sugar
1 teaspoon soft brown sugar
1 tablespoon white wine vinegar
2 tablespoons water
salt and freshly ground pepper

110g plain flour
2 teaspoons baking powder
1 teaspoon chilli powder
2 organic eggs, beaten
150ml water
4 onions, thinly sliced in rings
2 tablespoons snipped fresh chives
sunflower oil

First make the sauce. Put the chillies, pepper, tomatoes and garlic into a stainless steel saucepan with the sugars, vinegar and water. Season and simmer for 10 minutes until reduced by half.

Sieve the flour, baking powder and chilli powder into a bowl. Make a well in the centre, add the eggs, gradually add in the water, mix to make a smooth batter. Stir in the thinly sliced onions and chives. Season well with salt and freshly ground pepper.

Just before serving heat the oil to 170°C approximately.

Fry teaspoons of the batter in the sunflower oil for about 5 minutes on each side until crisp and golden, drain on kitchen paper. Serve hot or cold with the tomato and chilli sauce.

SIDE

CHEESY KALE GRATIN

Preheat the oven to 190°C/gas mark 5. Remove the stalks from **250g kale** and shred finely. Plunge into boiling water for 30-60 seconds, then refresh under cold water. Set aside. Melt **25g butter** in a saucepan, stir in **25g plain flour** and cook for 2 minutes. Remove the pan from the heat and gradually blend in **450ml full fat organic milk**, stirring well. Place back on the heat and bring gently to the boil, stirring continuously until thickened and smooth. Crumble in **125g goat's cheese**. Add **½ teaspoon mustard powder** and **salt** and **freshly ground black pepper**, and mix well. Place the kale in an ovenproof dish, then spoon over the sauce. Combine **75g breadcrumbs** and **1 tablespoon caraway seeds**, then spread evenly over the surface. Bake in the oven for 20-25 minutes or until the topping is golden brown. Serves 4-6

DINNER

LEEK, POTATO AND FETA 'PIZZETTA'

SERVES 4

A pizzetta is simply a small pizza. The puff pastry in this recipe is a shortcut but it produces a highly satisfactory result. If you can't find Charlotte potatoes, use another waxy variety.

250g potatoes, cut into slices about 5mm thick
2 tablespoons olive oil
4 leeks, trimmed and finely sliced
500g puff pastry
100g feta
1 tablespoon fresh thyme leaves
sea salt and freshly ground black pepper

Preheat the oven to 200°C/gas mark 6.

Boil the potatoes until tender, about 10 minutes, then drain thoroughly.

Meanwhile heat the oil in a large frying pan, add the leeks, and cook on a medium heat until softened, about 7-8 minutes. Add the potatoes to the pan and season with salt and freshly ground black pepper, stir to combine and cook for a further 1-2 minutes.

On a lightly-floured surface, roll out the puff pastry in a circle roughly 25cm in diameter, to a thickness of about 5mm. Place the pastry on a large baking tray and, using a sharp knife, lightly score a border 5mm in from the edge.

Spoon the leek and potato mixture over the pastry, leaving the 5mm border. Crumble over the feta, sprinkle over the thyme, then bake in the oven for 30 minutes until the edges of the pastry are golden. If the top is browning, cover with foil then return to the oven.

DESSERT

BAKED PEARS

Preheat the oven to 180°C/gas mark 4. Tip **50g whole almonds** into a small roasting tin and toast in the oven for 5 minutes. Leave to cool slightly and then roughly chop the almonds and tip them into a bowl. Crumble **6 soft amaretti biscuits** and add to the chopped almonds with the **zest of 1 lemon** and **a pinch of ground cinnamon**. In another small bowl cream together **75g softened unsalted butter** and **1 tablespoon golden caster sugar** until pale and light. Add **1 organic egg yolk** and **a teaspoon of vanilla extract** and beat again until smooth before adding the crumbled biscuit mixture. Peel **4 ripe pears** using a vegetable peeler and toss in the **juice of 1 lemon** to prevent them discolouring. Halve the pears and remove the cores using a melon baller, and arrange in a greased ovenproof dish cut side uppermost. Stuff the pears with the filling mixture and pour over the remaining lemon juice. Drizzle over **4-6 tablespoons Marsala** and a couple of tablespoons of water, cover loosely with foil and bake on the middle shelf of the preheated oven for about 25 minutes or until tender. The cooking time will depend on the ripeness of the pears. Serve 2 pear halves per person with the buttery Marsala pan juices poured over and with a scoop of good quality vanilla ice cream or thick pouring cream. Serves 2

WEEK 08

BREAKFAST
FRENCH TOAST

Beat **4 organic eggs** lightly with a fork in a bowl. Stir in **1 teaspoon golden caster sugar, a pinch of salt,** and **250ml organic milk**. Melt a knob of **butter** in a non-stick frying pan set over a medium-low heat. Cut **8 slices of white bread** and dip them, one at a time, into the egg mixture. Soak only as many slices as you will be cooking at one time. Place the bread in the frying pan and cook gently until golden brown, then turn and brown the other side. Serve hot with **butter** and **syrup**. Serves 2

PACKED LUNCH
BLACK-EYED BEAN CASSEROLE WITH CORIANDER

Soak **250g black-eyed beans** in water overnight, drain and boil in plenty of water until tender, approximately 45 minutes. Heat **2 tablespoons sunflower oil** in a pan and cook **1 finely chopped onion** until golden brown. Add **2 finely chopped garlic cloves** just as the onions are browning. Add **1 tablespoon paprika, 1 bird's eye chilli** (deseeded and finely chopped) and **125g diced carrots** and cook slowly until the carrots are al dente. Pour in a **400g can chopped tomatoes** and the drained black-eyes beans and simmer gently for 5 minutes. Add a **326g can of sweetcorn, a dash of tabasco** and **salt** and **freshly ground black pepper**, and continue to simmer for 6–7 minutes making sure that it does not dry out. Remove from the heat and sprinkle over **a handful of finely chopped coriander**. Make a topping cream by mixing together **125ml soured cream,** approximately **10g roughly chopped coriander** and **1 tablespoon lime juice**. Season to taste before adding to the casserole. Serves 4

LUNCH
TORTILLA DE PATATAS
OMAR ALLIBHOY

SERVES 4

This is the classic Spanish tortilla, slowly fried on one side then turned over and fried on the other. Leaving the cooked potatoes in the egg mix for a while before using them helps soften them and unites them with the rest of the dish.

1kg any good potatoes, finely chopped
    (3mm thick)
1 Spanish onion, finely chopped (3mm thick)
olive oil, for frying
a pinch of table salt
10 organic eggs
aioli to serve

Fry the potatoes and onion in the olive oil over a high heat till golden (around 12–15 minutes) stirring them from time to time so they cook evenly. Drain them and mix them with the eggs and season with a pinch of salt. If you have the time, leave the mix soaking for at least 30 minutes.

To make the tortilla place a non-stick pan over a medium heat and drizzle in a bit of olive oil. Pour the tortilla mix inside the pan and lower the heat to a minimum. After 5 minutes, cover the pan with a plate (always wider than the pan) and, holding it tight with your hand, flip the side of the tortilla and slide it back into the pan. (Note: if it is the first time you flip a tortilla, you had better practice with the plate and an empty pan first). Depending on the size and depth of the pan in relation to the amount of tortilla mix, it will take longer or shorter to cook. I recommend eating the tortilla when still runny in the middle. Serve with aïoli.

SIDE

STUFFED ONIONS

For the stuffing, preheat the oven to 160°C/gas mark 3. Rub **6 slices of day-old wholemeal bread** into crumbs with your hands. Place the breadcrumbs in a shallow baking tin and bake in an oven until golden, approximately 10–15 minutes. Take out and allow to cool. In a large saucepan heat enough oil to cook **4 finely chopped sticks of celery** and **a few finely chopped sage leaves**, a **handful of thyme leaves** and **a sprig of rosemary leaves** over a moderate heat, until the celery is soft. Add **250g shelled and coarsely chopped chestnuts** and cook a further minute. Add **400g can lentils** and the breadcrumbs to the chestnut mix. Stir in **a handful of freshly chopped parsley**, **salt** and **freshly ground black pepper**. Let the stuffing cool completely. For the onions, chop off the tops and bottoms of **4 large red onions**, then peel. Use your hands to rub **a little oil** over surface of onions. Sprinkle with **freshly ground black pepper** and roast at 180°C/gas mark 4 for 20 minutes or until they start to soften. Take out of the oven and when cool enough to handle, push out the centres, leaving a hollow shell to take the stuffing. Chop up the rest of the onion and add to the stuffing. Fill the hollow onions with the stuffing. Sit the onion tops back on and bake in the oven for a further 30 minutes. Serves 4

DINNER

VEGETABLE SATAY

SERVES 4

The almonds here are a pleasing alternative to the peanuts on which most satays are based. The savoury sweetness of the sauce is matched by the same quality in the caramelised vegetables.

1 tablespoon sesame oil
1 tablespoon vegetable oil
1 red chilli, deseeded and finely chopped
2 garlic cloves, crushed
2cm root ginger, finely grated
1/2 teaspoon turmeric
1 teaspoon tamarind paste
50g ground almonds

2 tablespoons peanut butter
350ml coconut milk
juice and zest from 1 lime
1 teaspoon sea salt
1–2 sweet potatoes
2–3 carrots
2–3 turnips

Heat the sesame and vegetable oil in a frying pan and fry the chilli, garlic, ginger, turmeric and tamarind paste. Add the ground almonds, peanut butter, coconut milk, lime juice and zest, salt and simmer for 2–3 minutes. Remove from the heat and leave to cool.

For the vegetables, preheat the oven to 180°C/gas mark 4. Peel the vegetables and cut into 2.5cm cubes. Marinate in the sauce for 5 minutes. Transfer the vegetables to a baking tray, cover with foil and bake for 25–30 minutes, until tender but barely coloured. Set aside to cool. Spear the vegetables onto skewers and cook, on a hot griddle, over a high heat until coloured. Heat through the remaining sauce and serve separately.

DESSERT

CHOCOLATE AND CHESTNUT CAKE

Preheat the oven to 180°C/gas mark 4. Grease the inside of a 20cm springform tin and line the base with a disc of buttered baking parchment. Dust with **1 tablespoon cocoa** and tip out the excess. Tip **200g pre-cooked, peeled chestnuts** into a small frying pan, add **2 tablespoons caster sugar** and **100ml full fut organic milk** and cook over a low-medium heat for 5 minutes until the chestnuts start to soften. Remove from the heat and tip into the bowl of a food-processor and whizz until smooth. Add **1 teaspoon vanilla extract** and cool. Place **100g unsalted butter** and **150g chopped dark chocolate** in a heatproof bowl and melt either in the microwave on a low setting or over a pan of barely simmering water. Stir until smooth, remove from the heat and cool slightly. Whisk **3 large organic eggs** and **75g caster sugar** until thick, pale and doubled in volume. Mix in the chestnuts until thoroughly combined. Add the melted chocolate mixture and fold in until smooth. Carefully pour the batter into the prepared tin, spread level and bake on the middle shelf of the preheated oven for about 30 minutes until risen and the top has formed a light crust. Remove the cake from the oven and set the tin on a wire cooling rack and leave to cool to room temperature. The cake will sink and the crust might crack as it cools but this is part of the cake's appeal. Dust with **cocoa** and serve with **crème fraîche**. Serves 4

WEEK 09

BREAKFAST

WINTER FRUIT SALAD

Take **150g dried apricots** and **170g prunes** and soak them overnight covered in boiling water. Put into a casserole in the morning and add **2 tablespoons currants** and the **zest of a small lemon**. Mix in **2 tablespoons honey** and double the quantity of water. Bring the pan to the boil and then simmer for about 25–30 minutes. Cool and refrigerate. Before serving for breakfast the next day, add **175ml orange juice** and **2 sliced bananas**. Serve with **Greek yogurt** if you like.

PACKED LUNCH

GREEN PEA PILAU

Heat **125ml vegetable oil** in a large saucepan over a moderate heat and finely chop **1 small onion**. Fry the chopped onion, **broken cinnamon stick, 1 teaspoon freshly chopped ginger, 1/2 teaspoon chilli powder, a pinch of ground turmeric, 1/2 teaspoon cumin seeds** and **1 teaspoon salt** for 10 minutes. Add **750ml water** and bring to the boil. Add **375g long grain rice**, cover, lower the heat and simmer for 15 minutes. Add **250g frozen peas** and cook for a further 5 minutes, until all the liquid has been absorbed and the rice is tender and fluffy. Serves 6

LUNCH

SPICED WHOLEWHEAT COUSCOUS WITH SWEET POTATO AND PISTACHIOS

STELLA McCARTNEY

SERVES 4

Wholewheat couscous is nuttier and that little bit more nutritious than the white, bran-free variety. It complements sweet potato perfectly and vice versa. This is a typical North African dish; za'tar is a spice mix used extensively in the region's cookery.

3 small sweet potatoes
4 tablespoons olive oil
2 tablespoons pumpkin seeds
150g giant wholewheat couscous
500ml light vegetable stock or water
handful of raisins, preferably organic
1 rounded teaspoon za'tar
50g unshelled, unsalted pistachios, chopped

TO SERVE
1 lemon
2 tablespoons extra virgin olive oil
2 tablespoons freshly chopped coriander
2 tablespoons freshly chopped flatleaf parsley
1 tablespoon freshly chopped mint
salt and freshly ground black pepper

Preheat the oven to 200°C/gas mark 6.

Scrub the sweet potatoes under cold water and cut each into 6 wedges. Tip into a roasting tin, drizzle with 2 tablespoons of olive oil, season with salt and freshly ground black pepper, and roast in the oven for about 20–25 minutes or until the sweet potato is tender and starting to caramelise at the edges. Add the pumpkin seeds to the pan for the last 5 minutes of cooking time.

While the sweet potato is cooking prepare the couscous. Heat 2 tablespoons olive oil in a large sauté pan, add the couscous and cook gently for 2–3 minutes until starting to brown. Add half of the stock or water to the pan and continue to cook for about 15 minutes, stirring frequently until the couscous is tender and has absorbed the liquid. Add the remaining stock or water to the pan as and when needed. Add the raisins, za'tar and chopped pistachios to the pan, season with salt and freshly ground black pepper and cool slightly.

Mix together the juice from half the lemon and the extra virgin olive oil and pour over the warm sweet potato when it comes out of the oven. Gently stir the freshly chopped herbs and roasted sweet potato wedges into the couscous and serve with extra lemon wedges for squeezing over.

SIDE

COLCANNON

Mash **500g peeled and cooked** potatoes and season with **salt** and **freshly ground black pepper** before stirring in the **slices of 1 cooked leek** and juices in which they were cooked. Then add **500g sliced and cooked cabbage** and mix thoroughly over a low heat. Arrange on a warmed serving dish and make a hole in the centre. Keep warm. Partly melt **4 tablespoons butter**, season, and pour it into the cavity. Serve immediately. Serves 4

DINNER

GLAMORGAN SAUSAGES

The McCartney family knows a fair bit about vegetarian sausages — Linda's are the UK's best-selling brand — but the Welsh have been making this excellent cheese-based variety for at least 150 years. Describing them as sausages may be stretching a point, as they don't have skins, but however you classify them they are extremely good. The ideal cheese to use is Caerphilly, which is delightfully fresh and crumbly.

25g butter
1 large onion, finely chopped
1 leek, trimmed and finely sliced
1 garlic clove, crushed
250g fresh white breadcrumbs
1/2 teaspoon dry mustard powder
2 tablespoons freshly chopped parsley

100g Welsh cheese, such as Caerphilly, crumbled or grated
2 large organic eggs, beaten
2 tablespoons plain flour
2 tablespoons vegetable oil
salt and freshly ground black pepper

SERVES 4

Melt the butter in a small frying pan and gently fry the onions and leeks for 3–4 minutes until just softened. Add the crushed garlic and cook for a further 30 seconds. Transfer the vegetables to a bowl and mix with the breadcrumbs, mustard, parsley, cheese and a good sprinkling of salt and freshly ground black pepper.

Bind the mixture together with the beaten eggs. Divide into 8 and form into sausage shapes or small patties. Lightly roll into the flour.

Heat the oil in a frying pan and gently fry the 'sausages' or cakes for 3–4 minutes on each side until golden brown. Drain on kitchen paper and serve immediately.

DESSERT

PEAR CAKE

Preheat the oven to 160°C/gas mark 3. Grease and line the base of a 20cm round tin. Grind **100g blanched hazelnuts** in a food-processor until fairly fine. Add **140g self-raising flour** and mix. Add **175g butter** chopped into small pieces and pulse until it forms crumbs. Add **140g golden caster sugar** and **2 beaten large organic eggs** and mix briefly. Peel, core and chop **2 small ripe Conference pears** and stir into the mixture. Spoon the mixture into the tin and smooth the top. Peel, core and slice **3 small ripe Conference pears** and scatter over the top of the cake. Press down lightly and bake for 50-60 minutes until firm to the touch. Cool in the tin for 10 minutes, then turn out and cool on a wire rack. Serves 8

WEEK 10

BREAKFAST

DRIED APRICOT COMPOTE

Put **2 tablespoons freshly squeezed lemon juice**, **125ml freshly squeezed orange juice** and **2 tablespoons runny honey** in a small pan and bring gently to the boil. Then add **250g dried apricots** and **125g raisins**. Reduce the heat and simmer them until tender — about 10 minutes. Remove the fruits and boil up the liquid for a couple of minutes to reduce it. Put the fruits back into the sauce, together with **100g chopped toasted walnuts**, and serve either warm or refrigerate and serve well chilled. Serves 4

PACKED LUNCH

FARRO, SUN-DRIED TOMATOES AND FETA

MINDY FOX

Bring a medium saucepan of salted water to the boil. Add **280g dried farro** and cook for about 18 minutes until tender but still firm to the bite. Drain and transfer to a bowl. Add **3 tablespoons good-quality extra virgin olive oil**, then finely grate **the zest of 1 lemon** into the bowl, holding the zester close to catch any flavourful oil from the rind. Toss to combine. Add **70g sheep's milk feta**, **1 tablespoon sun-dried tomato spread** (or finely chopped sun-dried tomatoes in oil), **10g roughly chopped parsley** and **a few generous pinches of flaky coarse sea salt**. Stir to combine. Allow the flavours to meld for a couple of minutes, then taste and adjust the amounts of sun-dried tomato spread and salt to your liking. Serve warm or at room temperature. Serves 4

LUNCH

POTATO AND PEA SAMOSAS

SERVES 4

Samosas can take almost any filling you can dream up but this potato and pea combination proves that simple is often best. Make sure you make a large batch.

400g potatoes, peeled and cut into 1cm dice
150g frozen peas, cooked and drained
1/2 teaspoon cumin seeds
1/2 teaspoon coriander seeds
seeds from 4 cardamon pods
1/2 teaspoon black onion seeds
2 tablespoons sunflower oil
1 onion, finely chopped
1 fat garlic clove, crushed
1/2 tablespoon freshly grated ginger

1 large green chilli, deseeded and finely chopped
1/2 teaspoon turmeric powder
1/4 teaspoon chilli powder
1 rounded tablespoon mango chutney
2 tablespoons chopped coriander
270g filo pastry
melted butter, to brush
salt and freshly ground black pepper

Cook the potatoes in boiling salted water until tender. Add the peas and cook for a further 30 seconds. Drain and set aside. Tip the cumin, coriander and cardamon into a frying pan and toast over a medium heat for 1 minute. Coarsely grind the onion seeds using a pestle and mortar.

Heat the oil in a large frying pan, add the onion and cook until soft. Add the garlic, ginger and chilli and cook for 30 seconds then add the spices. Continue to cook for 1 minute, then add the diced potatoes and peas. Mix well and cook for 3–4 minutes, stirring frequently. Remove from the heat, add the chutney and chopped coriander and season well.

Preheat the oven to 190°C/gas mark 5. Lay a sheet of filo pastry on the work surface and brush with melted butter. Lay another pastry sheet on top and cut into strips 7cm wide then brush with the melted butter. Put a spoonful of the potato mixture onto the top left hand corner of each strip. Fold over to make a triangle and continue folding down the length of the strip to completely encase the filling. Repeat with the remaining filling and pastry. Arrange on baking trays and bake for 25 minutes until golden and crisp. Serve with pickles and relishes.

SIDE

TANGY ROOTS

Preheat the oven to 180°C/gas mark 4. Place **1 chopped parsnip** and **1 trimmed and chopped leek** in a roasting tin, add **10g fresh thyme leaves** and **salt** and **freshly ground black pepper**. Dot with **50g butter** and cook in the preheated oven for 10 minutes, stirring once. Add **2 diced carrots** and cook for a further 30 minutes, until just tender. Add **200g peeled and cooked chestnuts**, **1/2 shredded Savoy cabbage**, **1 tablespoon Seville marmalade** and **150ml vegetable stock** and cook for a further 10 minutes. Serve hot. Serves 4

DINNER

VEGETARIAN LASAGNE

SERVES 4

Vegetable lasagne is a student staple but it can be a whole lot better than that implies. The key is to take a bit of care and follow a decent recipe like this one.

3 tablespoons olive oil
1 aubergine, cut into rounds 1cm thick
1 large courgette, cut into slices
250g ball mozzarella, drained
8–10 dry lasagne sheets
2 tablespoons freshly grated vegetarian Parmesan

FOR THE CHEESE SAUCE
30g butter
30g plain flour
550ml organic milk
100g grated Gruyère
salt and freshly ground black pepper

FOR THE TOMATO SAUCE
1–2 tablespoons olive oil
1 onion, finely chopped
2 garlic cloves, finely chopped
1 tablespoon tomato purée
400g can tomatoes
150g cherry tomatoes, halved
1 teaspoon sugar
2 tablespoons freshly chopped basil leaves

Preheat the oven to 200°C/gas mark 6. Heat 1 tablespoon of olive oil in a large frying pan over a high heat, add the aubergine slices in a single layer and sauté until golden brown on both sides. Repeat with the remaining aubergine and the courgette adding more oil to the pan as needed.

Prepare the tomato sauce. Heat the olive oil in a saucepan, add the onion and cook until soft but not coloured. Add the garlic and continue to cook for 1 minute. Add the tomato purée with both the tomatoes and the sugar and season with salt and freshly ground black pepper. Cook over a low-medium heat for 20 minutes until the sauce has reduced and thickened slightly. Check the seasoning, add the basil, remove from the heat and cool slightly.

Prepare the cheese sauce. Melt the butter in a saucepan. Stir in the flour and cook for 2 minutes. Slowly add the milk to the pan, stirring constantly. Bring to the boil and simmer very gently for 3–4 minutes stirring constantly until the sauce has thickened, coats the back of a spoon and is smooth and glossy. Remove from the heat and stir in the Gruyère.

Spoon half of the tomato sauce into the base of a 20 x 30 cm ovenproof dish. Scatter with half of the aubergine and courgettes. Tear half of the mozzarella into pieces and scatter over the vegetables and top with a layer of lasagne sheets. Repeat this layering one more time. Spoon the cheese sauce over the final lasagne layer, scatter with grated vegetarian Parmesan and bake for about 30 minutes until golden and bubbling.

DESSERT

CREME BRULEE

Preheat the oven to 150°C/gas mark 2. Mix **6 organic egg yolks** with **3 tablespoons golden caster sugar**. Heat **568ml double cream** and **1 vanilla pod** to just below boiling then leave for 30 minutes to infuse. Reheat and whisk into the egg mixture. Strain the custard into 4 small ramekins. Sit the ramekins in a small roasting tin and pour hot water into the tin to come halfway up the ramekins. Bake for 20–30 minutes until the custards are just set but still wobbly in the centre. Cool, then chill for at least 2 hours (preferably overnight). To finish, sprinkle the top of each custard with a layer of **caster sugar**, about 1 tablespoon per pot, then place under an extremely hot grill until the surface is golden and caramelised. Serves 4

WEEK 11

BREAKFAST

TOFU SCRAMBLE WITH SPINACH

Drain and slice **1 block of tofu** into 2.5cm cubes, then, crumble it slightly. Sauté **½ diced onion** and the crumbled tofu in **oil** for 3-5 minutes, stirring often. Add **2 tablespoons vegetable oil**, **1 tablespoon soy sauce**, **½ teaspoon turmeric** and **salt** and **freshly ground black pepper** and reduce the heat to medium and allow to cook for 5 minutes, stirring frequently and adding more oil if necessary. Add **100g spinach** and let it wilt for 2 minutes. Serve topped with **grated cheese** or wrapped in a **warmed tortilla** with **1 teaspoon of salsa** for a breakfast burrito. Serves 2

SIDE

SMOKY POLENTA CHIPS

YOTAM OTTOLENGHI

Line a shallow tray with clingfilm. Bring **375ml vegetable stock** to the boil in a saucepan. Slowly add **60g quick-cook polenta** while stirring with a wooden spoon. Cook on a gentle heat for 5 minutes, stirring all the time. Remove from the heat and mix in **20g butter**, **60g grated scarmorza affuicata cheese** and **salt** and **freshly ground black pepper** to taste. Once the cheese and butter have melted into the mix, transfer it to the lined tray. Use a wet spatula to level the polenta to an even 5mm. Cover the surface with clingfilm and leave to cool completely, then chill for at least 30 minutes. Meanwhile, make a tomato sauce. Place a large non-stick frying pan on high heat. Once hot, add **350g plum tomatoes** and leave for about 15 minutes, stirring occasionally. The tomato skins need to blacken well; don't remove them from the heat too early. Transfer the hot tomatoes to a mixing bowl and break them with a spoon. Pick out the skins and discard. Heat **2 tablespoons olive oil** in a small pan, add **½ thinly sliced medium onion** and cook on medium heat for 3 minutes, just to soften. Add the onion and oil to the tomatoes, then add **2 crushed garlic cloves**, **a pinch of chilli flakes**, **¼ teaspoon caster sugar** and **salt** to taste. Leave on the side until the sauce comes to room temperature and then stir in **2 tablespoons chopped parsley** if you like. Once properly set remove the polenta from the tray and cut it into chips, roughly 1.5cm thick and 6cm long. Fill a medium saucepan with enough vegetable oil to come 2cm up its sides and heat well. Toss the chips in **plain flour** until well coated, shake off the excess and carefully place in hot **vegetable oil**. Fry for about 3 minutes to a golden-brown colour and transfer to a kitchen towel. Don't fry too many chips at a time. Serve the hot chips with the tomato sauce spooned on top or in a bowl on the side. Serves 4

LUNCH

RICH AND CREAMY CELERIAC GRATIN

SERVES 4

Celeriac has a slightly nutty, milder and sweeter taste than celery — ideal for making a rich and creamy gratin.

25g butter
1kg celeriac, peeled and thinly sliced
4 garlic cloves, finely chopped
2 fresh red chillies, finely chopped

1 large sprig rosemary leaves, finely chopped
100g Cheddar
salt and freshly ground black pepper
500ml single cream

Preheat the oven to 190°C/gas mark 5. Butter a large gratin dish. Cover the base of the gratin dish with a layer of celeriac. Scatter over some of the garlic, chilli, rosemary and cheese, and season with salt and pepper. Repeat the layers until everything has been used up, ending with celeriac but reserving a little of the cheese to go on the top. Pour over just enough cream to reach the last layer — it shouldn't cover the celeriac. Sprinkle over the reserved cheese, dot with butter and bake for 40–50 minutes, until crisp and golden and the celeriac can be easily pierced with a fork.

SIDE
CITRUS BASMATI RICE

Cook **300g basmati rice** for 15-20 minutes or according to the packet instructions until cooked through. Stir in the **zest and juice of 1 lime**, **zest and juice of 1 lemon**, **20g finely chopped coriander**, **100ml natural yogurt**, adding **salt** and **freshly ground black pepper** to taste. Serve immediately, garnished with **lime wedges** and some **coriander leaves**. Serves 4

DINNER
PUMPKIN AND TOFU LAKSA

SERVES 4

Laksa is a Malaysian dish consisting of noodles served in a spicy, coconut milk-based broth. The silky tofu in this recipe ameliorates the heat, as do the matchsticks of cucumber sprinkled over the top of the dish to serve.

250g pumpkin of your choice, deseeded and cut into 1cm dice
4 tablespoons vegetable oil
250g tofu, cut into 4 equal pieces
750ml coconut milk
3 tablespoons soy sauce
2 teaspoons sugar
200g rice noodles
150g beansprouts
1 cucumber, deseeded and cut into matchsticks
3-4 spring onions, trimmed and cut into matchsticks

1 small bunch coriander, leaves only
sea salt

FOR THE SPICE PASTE
2 garlic cloves, crushed
1 red chilli, finely chopped
1 tablespoon finely grated fresh ginger
3-4 spring onions, finely chopped
1 teaspoon turmeric
1 stalk lemongrass
3 lime leaves, chopped
juice of 1 lime

Put the pumpkin in a saucepan, cover with water, add a pinch of salt and bring to the boil. Reduce the heat, cover with a lid, and simmer for 10 minutes until the pumpkin is tender and can be pierced easily with a fork. Drain, reserving the cooking liquid, and keep warm.

Put all the ingredients for the spice paste in a blender, together with 1-2 tablespoons of water, and blitz until you have a smooth, but not too thick, purée.

Heat 1 tablespoon of oil in a frying pan set over a medium heat, add the tofu and fry until golden, about 3-4 minutes. Remove from the pan and set aside.

Heat 2 tablespoons of oil in a saucepan, add the spice paste and fry for 2-3 minutes. Then add the coconut milk, tofu, soy sauce and sugar, followed by the reserved pumpkin liquid. Bring to the boil, reduce the heat and simmer for 10-15 minutes until the liquid has thickened slightly.

Meanwhile, put the noodles in a bowl, cover with boiling water and let them soak for 10 minutes, stirring them occasionally so they don't stick together. Drain thoroughly, toss in the remaining oil, and divide between four warmed bowls. Top each with beansprouts and pumpkin cubes and a piece of tofu. Ladle over the coconut liquid and scatter with the cucumber, onions and coriander.

DESSERT
BROWNIES

Preheat the oven to 170°C/gas mark 3. Grease and line a 20 x 30cm baking tin with baking parchment. Tip **100g walnut halves** onto a baking sheet and toast in the oven for 5 minutes, leave to cool, then roughly chop. Melt **150g diced unsalted butter** and **225g chopped dark chocolate** together in a heatproof bowl either in the microwave on a low setting or over a pan of barely simmering water. Remove from the heat, stir until smooth and cool slightly. In another bowl whisk together **4 large beaten organic eggs**, **300g golden caster sugar** and **1 teaspoon vanilla extract**. Add the melted chocolate and butter mixture and whisk gently until combined. Sift **125g plain flour** and **a pinch of salt** into the bowl and fold into the batter along with the chopped nuts. Pour into the prepared tin, spread level and bake on the middle shelf of the preheated oven for 25 minutes until the top has formed a light crust and the underneath is still slightly squidgy. Cool in the tin and then cut into squares to serve. Makes 9 squares

WEEK 12

BREAKFAST

TOASTED BAGEL WITH HUMMUS

PAUL McCARTNEY

My favourite breakfast – not only quick and easy, but also very nutritious. Split **a bagel** in half and lightly toast. Spread one half with **½ teaspoon Marmite or Vegemite** and the other with **1 tablespoon hummus** (either shop bought or see page 23), then sandwich together. Delicious!

PACKED LUNCH

BLOOD ORANGE, AVOCADO AND BUTTERBEAN SALAD

ALLEGRA McEVEDY

Using a small sharp knife, cut the top and bottom off **2 blood oranges** and sit them on a chopping board. Working from top to bottom, and following the shape of the orange, cut the peel off in sections. Pick up your naked orange and, over a little bowl, cut between the white dividers so that the orange segments fall into the bowl. Once you have cut out all the segments, give the remaining pulp a good squeeze so that all the juice falls into the bowl. Chop up the stalky ends of **a large handful of watercress** until you get to the leaves, and put both parts in a big bowl with the orange segments (but retain the juice), **1 sliced avocado**, **1 grated carrot**, **150g cooked butterbeans** and **a handful of mint leaves**. Measure out 5 tablespoons of the orange juice into a mug (you can drink any remaining juice) with **3 tablespoons extra virgin olive oil** and **1 tablespoon red wine vinegar**. Season with **salt and freshly ground black pepper**, give it a quick whisk with a fork then spoon it over the salad. Serves 2

LUNCH

CLASSIC FRENCH ONION SOUP

SERVES 4

This is the definitive French soup, rich, filling and moreish. Slow cooking the onions gives them tremendous depth of flavour and gives the soup its lovely amber colour. The cheese-topped croûtons are simply ace.

1 tablespoon sunflower oil
50g butter
500g onions, thinly sliced
150ml white wine

750ml vegetable stock
4 thick slices stone baked baguette
100g Gruyère, grated
sea salt and freshly ground black pepper

Melt the oil and butter in a heavy-bottomed saucepan, add the onions and cook, stirring occasionally, until the edges of the onions begin to turn dark. Reduce the heat to very low and continue to cook the onions for a further 30 minutes until they are a rich brown colour.

Raise the heat, pour in the wine and deglaze the pan, scraping the base and edges well. Pour in the stock, season with salt and freshly ground pepper, bring to a simmer and leave to cook very gently for about 45 minutes.

When ready to serve, toast the slices of baguette, sprinkle thickly with the Gruyère and place under a grill until the cheese is melted. Place each piece of toast in 4 individual bowls, ladle over the soup and serve.

SIDE/SNACK

CRISP AND GOLDEN POORIS

Place **150g plain wholemeal flour** and **½ teaspoon salt** in a bowl, add **125ml water** and mix to a fairly soft dough. Knead for 4–5 minutes, until soft but no longer sticky. Turn the dough onto a lightly-floured surface, and work and roll it with your hands until you have a long snake of dough, about 2cm in diameter. Cut off a piece of dough about 2cm long, and wrap the remaining dough in clingfilm. Work the cut off piece of dough between your palms until it forms a small, neat ball. Coat with **flour**, then roll out until you have a small, flat patty about 8cm in diameter. Continue cutting and shaping the dough in this way, always keeping the pieces of dough covered with clingfilm when not being worked. Heat **250ml vegetable oil** in a wok or large frying pan until hot enough to brown a cube of bread in 30 seconds, and deep fry the pooris, 1 or 2 at a time, making sure you don't overcrowd the pan. Cook each batch for 2–3 minutes, until lightly browned, turning them once and splashing them with hot oil to make them puff up. Drain on kitchen paper before serving warm. Makes 14

DINNER

SWEET POTATO JALFREZI

SERVES 4

Jalfrezi has recently displaced tikka masala as the UK's favourite kind of curry. It is quite hot but in this recipe the juiciness of the mango cools it down delightfully.

1–2 tablespoons vegetable oil
1 medium onion, chopped
1 garlic clove, crushed
2 tablespoons Jalfrezi seasoning
600ml vegetable stock
300ml passata

500g sweet potatoes, chopped into 1cm dice
500g cauliflower, broken into small florets
1 red pepper, deseeded and cut into 1cm strips
1 mango, peeled and roughly chopped
2 tablespoons chopped coriander
salt and freshly ground black pepper

Heat the oil in a heavy-bottomed pan. Gently cook the onion and garlic until soft. Stir in the Jalfrezi seasoning and cook for 3 minutes. Stir in the stock, passata, sweet potatoes, cauliflower and pepper. Bring to the boil, reduce the heat and simmer until the vegetables are tender.

Season to taste. Stir in the mango and coriander and serve immediately. Rice and slices of mango make an ideal accompaniment.

DESSERT

ALMOND SWEETS

Place **75g stoned dates, 75g dried apricots, 50g seedless raisins** and **2 tablespoons apple juice** in a food-processor or blender and work together until smooth, scraping down the sides as necessary. Form the mixture into balls the size of a cherry, then roll them in **50g chopped and browned almonds** until completely coated. Makes 30

WEEK 13

BREAKFAST

CINNAMON RAISIN TOAST

Beat **4 organic eggs** lightly with a fork in a bowl. Stir in **1 teaspoon demerara sugar**, **a pinch of salt** and **250ml organic milk**. Melt **a knob of butter** in a non-stick frying pan set over a medium-low heat. Dip **8 slices of white bread**, one at a time, into the egg mixture. Soak only as many slices as you will be cooking at 1 time. Place the bread in the frying pan and cook gently until golden brown, then turn and brown the other side. Scatter over **a handful of raisins**, dust with **ground cinnamon** and drizzle over some **honey** if you wish. Serves 2

PACKED LUNCH

ROASTED VEG AND GIANT WHOLEWHEAT COUSCOUS SALAD

Preheat the grill. Halve and deseed **3 red peppers** and place cut-side down on a baking tray. Place under the grill and char until the skins are blackened. Put the peppers in a plastic bag and seal. When cool enough to handle, remove the skins, cut into strips, drizzle with **1 tablespoon olive oil** and set aside. Thinly slice **2 onions** and place on another baking tray. Drizzle with **1 tablespoon olive oil**, season with **salt** and **freshly ground black pepper**, and grill, turning occasionally, until charred at the edges. Set aside. Bring a pan of water to the boil, add **100g giant wholewheat couscous**, and simmer for 7 minutes. Drain then tip into a bowl. Add the roasted peppers and onions and **50g sliced marinated artichoke hearts**. Whisk together **2 tablespoons olive oil** with **1 tablespoon balsamic vinegar** and stir into the couscous. Serves 2

LUNCH

WINTER MINESTRONE

STELLA McCARTNEY

SERVES 4

Don't be fooled by the name — the character of this thick, wholesome soup is more North African than Italian. It has a lot in common with the European version though, with the couscous playing a similar role to the vermicelli noodles found in many recipes.

200g farro semiperlato (or pearled spelt)
4 tablespoons olive oil, plus extra to serve
1 large onion, finely chopped
1 leek, finely chopped
1 stick celery, finely chopped
2 medium carrots, peeled and finely chopped
1 medium turnip, peeled and finely chopped
3 garlic cloves, crushed

pinch of crushed dried chilli flakes
400g can tomatoes
800ml – 1 litre vegetable stock
400g can cannellini beans, drained and rinsed
1 bunch cavolo nero, shredded
salt and freshly ground black pepper
freshly grated vegetarian Parmesan to serve

Rinse the farro in a sieve under cold running water, tip into a bowl, cover with cold water and soak for 20 minutes while you prepare the soup base. Heat the olive oil in a large saucepan. Add the chopped veggies and cook over a low-medium heat for 10–15 minutes until tender but not coloured. Add the crushed garlic and chilli flakes and cook for a further minute.

Pour the tomatoes into the pan, add the stock and bring to the boil. Drain the farro and add to the pan. Reduce the heat to a gentle simmer, cover and cook the soup for 25 minutes until the vegetables are tender and the farro is cooked. Add the cannellini beans and cook for a further 2–3 minutes. You may need to add extra stock if the soup is too thick. Add the cavolo nero and cook for 3–4 minutes until tender.

Season to taste with salt and freshly ground black pepper. Serve in bowls with a drizzle of olive oil, a scattering of grated Parmesan and slices of toasted sourdough bread.

SIDE

SPICED PARSNIPS

Preheat the oven to 220°C/gas mark 7. Cook **750g peeled and chopped parsnips** in boiling water for 2 minutes, then drain and toss in **50g melted butter or oil**. Mix together **3 tablespoons soft brown sugar**, **1 teaspoon ground cinnamon** and **1 teaspoon lemon zest**. Roll the buttered parsnips in the sugar mixture and bake in the oven for 20 minutes until golden. Serves 4

DINNER

VEGETARIAN SHEPHERD'S PIE

SERVES 4

There probably aren't that many vegetarian shepherds, unless they are responsible for sheep that are solely bred for their wool. Those that exist needn't feel disadvantaged compared to their carnivorous colleagues — they can make pies just as good based on Puy lentils and green split peas.

150g Puy lentils
100g green split peas
75g butter
1 red onion, chopped
2 carrots, chopped
2 sticks celery, chopped
1 garlic clove, finely chopped
1 tablespoon fresh thyme leaves
¼ teaspoon ground mace
¼ teaspoon cayenne pepper
75ml vegetable stock

3 medium size tomatoes, roughly chopped
700g floury potatoes
1 small onion, finely chopped
75g Cheddar, grated
2 tablespoons organic milk
sea salt
freshly ground black pepper

FOR THE TOMATO SAUCE
25g butter
200g tomatoes, skinned and chopped
1 tablespoon tomato ketchup

Preheat the oven to 190°C/gas mark 5.

Wash and pick over the lentils and split peas, put in a pan, cover with 350ml water and bring to the boil. Reduce the heat, cover and simmer gently until the lentils and peas have absorbed most of the water and are soft, about 40–45 minutes.

Melt 25g butter in a frying pan set over a medium heat and cook the red onion, carrots, celery and garlic until softened. Stir into the cooked lentils and split peas. Add the thyme, mace, and cayenne pepper, vegetable stock, and season with salt and freshly ground black pepper. Spoon into a 1 litre baking dish and arrange the slices of tomato in a layer on the top.

Peel and boil the potatoes until tender, then mash with 25g butter. Soften the onion in the remaining 25g butter and stir into the mash, along with the grated cheese and milk. Season with salt and freshly ground black pepper and spoon on top of the tomatoes. Place in the oven and bake for 30 minutes until golden.

To make the tomato sauce, melt the butter in a saucepan, then add the tomatoes and ketchup. Simmer on a low heat until thickened, about 15 minutes. Served spooned over the pie.

DESSERT

CHRISTMAS PUDDING TRIFLE

TRISTAN WELCH

Bring the **200ml organic milk** and **300ml double cream** to the boil with **a little nutmeg**. While the milk and cream are heating up whisk **6 organic egg yolks** and **70g sugar** together. Break up and divide a **Christmas pudding** into four 250ml jam jars. Once the milk and cream have boiled pour over the egg yolks and sugar constantly mixing. Once mixed, sieve the custard into the jars. Bake in the oven at 110°C/gas mark ¼ for 45 minutes. Once baked allow to chill in the fridge for a couple of hours. Top the jars with **8 crushed amaretti biscuits**, then **250ml double cream** whipped with **a dash of brandy** and then **a sprinkle of toasted almonds** to finish. Serves 4

RECIPE ACKNOWLEDGEMENTS

The publishers would like to thank the following for kind permission to reproduce their recipes:

SPRING

p.16   Spring Vegetable Tarte Fine by Tom Aikens

p.24   Limoncello and Ricotta Cheesecake by Gino D'Acampo (adapted from *The Italian Diet*, published by Kyle Books, 2010)

p.28   Spring Ragout of Artichoke Hearts, Broad Beans, Peas and Turnips by Stephanie Alexander (Excerpted from the UK edition of *Stephanie Alexander's Kitchen Garden Companion*, published by Quadrille, 2010)

p.40   Porcini and Celery Risotto by Theo Randall

p.43   Carrot and Hummus Crunch on Sourdough by Nick Sandler

p.44   Asparagus Tray Bake by Annie Bell

p.47   Creamy Broccoli Soup by Laura and Woody Harrelson

p.48   Linguine with Almonds and Caciocavallo by Mario Batali

p.55   Melon, Lime and Mint Soup by Stefan Gates (adapted from *The Extraordinary Cookbook* by Stefan Gates published by Kyle Books, 2010)

AUTUMN

p.124   Aubergine Casserole with Pomegranate by Maggie Beer

p.128   Roasted Butternut Squash and Marrow by Arthur Potts Dawson

p.148   Tomato, Feta, Almond and Date Baklava by Maria Elia

p.151   Pasta with Broccoli, Sun-dried Tomatoes and Olives by Livia Firth, Creative Director Eco-Age.com (http://Eco-Age.com)

p.155   Leek and Goat's Cheese Quiche by Bryn Williams

p.164   Whole Artichoke with Cobnut Dressing by Oliver Peyton

p.167   Mushroom, Mascarpone and Polenta Bake by Katie Caldesi

p.171   Spicy Tofu with Ginger by Josephine Fairley

p.172   Pizza Two Ways by Laura Bailey

SUMMER

p.70   Strawberries with Mascarpone and Cream by Pink

p.73   Broad Bean Salad with Cheese Chips by Giorgio Locatelli

p.77   Asparagus, Egg and Cress Sandwich by Tristan Welch

p.81   Carrot Soup by Anthony Demetre

p.82   Courgette Cakes by Fearne Cotton

p.90   Aubergine and Dried Apricot Pastilla by Bruno Loubet

p.93   Mozzarella Pasta by Twiggy

p.101   Pepper Pockets by James Tanner

p.102   Lentil Stew with Pan-fried Halloumi and Pomegranate by Kevin Spacey

p.106   Salad of Wild Rice, Charred Sweetcorn, Spiced Pecans, Avocado and Feta by Anna Hansen

p.109   Stilton Pâté with Melba Toast and Cherry Tomatoes by Andrew Maxwell

p.110   Paella Verduras by José Pizarro

p.113   Orange Marinated Tofu Skewers by Pamela Anderson

p.114   Potato and Gruyère Focaccia by Nick Malgieri

WINTER

p.177   Ale and Puff Pastry Pie by The Vegetarian Society

p.186   Winter Coleslaw by Vivienne Westwood

p.193   Chickpea Curry by Skye Gyngell

p.194   Potatoes with Hazelnuts and Rosemary by Simon Rogan

p.201   Onion Bhajis with Tomato and Chilli Sauce by Darina Allen

p.205   Tortilla de Patatas by Omar Allibhoy from Tapas Revolution

p.206   Stuffed Onions by Animal Aid

p.213   Farro, Sun-dried Tomatoes and Feta by Mindy Fox

p.217   Smoky Polenta Chips by Yotam Ottolenghi (first published in the *Guardian*)

p.221   Blood Orange, Avocado and Butterbean Salad by Allegra McEvedy

p.226   Christmas Pudding Trifle by Tristan Welch

FURTHER THANKS TO:

Paul, Mary and Stella McCartney, the team at Kyle Books, Claudia Tarry, Suzanne Barnard, John Hammel, Hanalei Perez-Lopez, Sam Merry, Sam Beckett, Stephane Jaspar, Stuart Bell, all at MPL.